## New Paternalism Meets Older Wisdom

## About IEA publications

The IEA publishes scores of books, papers, blogs and more – and much of this work is freely available from the IEA website: www.iea.org.uk

To access this vast resource, just scan the QR code below – it will take you directly to the IEA's Research home page.

*'Erik Matson has written a brilliant short book on behavioral economics and paternalism. He combines solid economic analysis with a deep knowledge of how the fundamental frameworks of David Hume and Adam Smith argue against paternalistic intervention. Today's advocates of the psychological foundations of economics would do well to read Matson's book.'*
    — Mario Rizzo, Professor of Economics, New York University

# NEW PATERNALISM MEETS OLDER WISDOM

## Looking to Smith and Hume on Rationality, Welfare and Behavioural Economics

ERIK W. MATSON

Institute of
**Economic** Affairs

First published in Great Britain in 2024 by
The Institute of Economic Affairs
2 Lord North Street
Westminster
London SW1P 3LB
in association with London Publishing Partnership Ltd
www.londonpublishingpartnership.co.uk

The mission of the Institute of Economic Affairs is to improve understanding of the fundamental institutions of a free society by analysing and expounding the role of markets in solving economic and social problems.

Copyright © The Institute of Economic Affairs 2024

The moral rights of the authors have been asserted.

All rights reserved. Without limiting the rights under copyright reserved above, no part of this publication may be reproduced, stored or introduced into a retrieval system, or transmitted, in any form or by any means (electronic, mechanical, photocopying, recording or otherwise), without the prior written permission of both the copyright owner and the publisher of this book.

A CIP catalogue record for this book is available from the British Library.

ISBN 978-0-255-36833-9

Many IEA publications are translated into languages other than English or are reprinted. Permission to translate or to reprint should be sought from the Director General at the address above.

Typeset in Kepler by T&T Productions Ltd
www.tandtproductions.com

Printed and bound by Hobbs the Printers Ltd

www.carbonbalancedprint.com
CBP2250

## CONTENTS

|   |   |
|---|---|
| *About the author* | vii |
| *List of figures* | vii |
| **Introductory remarks** | 1 |
| **1 Economics, psychology and the new paternalism** | **8** |
| The rise of behavioural economics | 8 |
| The new paternalism: origins and criticism | 18 |
| A bridge from the eighteenth century | 24 |
| **2 Our dynamic being within: Smithian challenges to the new paternalism** | **30** |
| Setting the stage | 31 |
| Smith on self-awareness and self-judgement | 34 |
| Self-approval and reasonable inconsistencies | 38 |
| Our dynamic being within | 50 |
| Error and affirmation | 56 |
| Implications and conclusions | 59 |
| **3 Satisfaction in action: Hume's endogenous theory of preferences and the virtues of commerce** | **63** |
| Hume on preferences | 66 |
| Pride and the sympathetic formation of preferences | 76 |
| Commerce and satisfaction in action | 88 |
| Conclusion | 100 |

## 4 The behavioural economist in society — 102
Dialoguing about happiness — 106
The political implications of Hume's happiness essays — 114
Hume's qualified theory of happiness — 118
Philosophy as a scene of conversation — 121
Conclusion — 127

## References — 129

## About the IEA — 148

## ABOUT THE AUTHOR

Erik W. Matson is a Senior Research Fellow at the Mercatus Center at George Mason University and a Lecturer in Political Economy in the Busch School of Business at The Catholic University of America. He serves as Deputy Director of the Adam Smith Program in the Department of Economics at George Mason. Focusing on the intellectual history and philosophy of early modern political economy, his research has been widely published in academic journals and edited volumes.

## FIGURES

| | | |
|---|---|---|
| Figure 1 | The four principal indirect passions | 80 |
| Figure 2 | The sympathetic formation of preferences | 86 |

For my mother

## INTRODUCTORY REMARKS

In recent decades, economics and related policy sciences have taken what might be called a 'behavioural turn'. Once-dominant theories of rationality and human behaviour have been enhanced, and in some cases replaced, by developments in fields such as neuroscience and experimental and cognitive psychology. These developments have yielded insights into human activity and decision-making processes. They have helped social and policy scientists better appreciate the complexity of rationality, the interplay between agent and environment, and the multi-faceted and social nature of the human person. Human beings are not simple, maximising, egoistical machines with a fixed set of preferences, as they have sometimes been modelled. To the contrary: we often lack well-formed preferences, and we do not always perceive a defined choice set over which to optimise; we are interested in conforming to rules and social expectations; our preferences are affected by narratives and situational framing; and we develop remarkably effective heuristics and mental shortcuts to navigate through complex situations about which we have very limited knowledge.[1] Such

---

1  To begin sampling the immense literature on these topics, consult Simon (1955), Kahneman et al. (1991), Bowles (1998), Smith (2003), Gigerenzer (2010) and Fehr and Hoff (2011).

perspectives are not new – many of them can be seen as a recovery of various understandings of human action dating back to classical antiquity, evidenced by the teachings of Aristotle, for example (cf. Bowles 2016). They came forth too, as will be discussed in the chapters below, in a major way in the writings of the Scottish Enlightenment. But they are now increasingly integrated into mainstream approaches to contemporary social sciences, including economics (Angner 2019).

This book is a collection of previously published essays, anchored in the history of economic thought, reflecting on some aspects of the behavioural turn. The behavioural turn in the social sciences has encompassed and continues to encompass a diverse array of approaches and research programmes. The target of the book is but a small subset of these: approaches that have aimed to use behavioural insights to design policies to make agents better off *as judged by their own subjective standards*. Such approaches have gone by different names: 'asymmetric paternalism' and 'regulation for conservatives' (Camerer et al. 2003), 'libertarian paternalism' (Sunstein and Thaler 2003a; Thaler and Sunstein 2009) and 'debiasing through law' (Jolls and Sunstein 2006). They are here grouped together under the heading of 'new paternalism'.

Whereas classical paternalism uses coercion to override agents' preferences for the sake of the agents' own good, the new paternalism proposes to use mechanism design and choice architecture to help agents do what the agents *themselves* want to do. Thus, one premise of the new paternalism is that agents will have difficulties doing what they really want. Intuitively, we each know that we struggle sometimes to do what we want – we smoke when we want to quit, we eat dessert when we want to diet, and so forth. Drawing on contemporary behavioural and psychological research, the new paternalists have a host of explanations *why*; so too do they have recommendations, based upon knowledge of our decision-making processes, to promote specific outcomes. If the goal is to increase savings rates and retirement account contributions, raise the default 401(k) contribution levels for employees instead of simply telling people to save more.[2] If the goal is to reduce smoking, use, in lieu of more traditional incentives (higher taxes), affective narratives (images on cigarette packs).

The new paternalism, as will be discussed below, came to prominence in the first decade of the 2000s. Some new paternalist proposals and formulations appear intuitive and non-controversial. But behind the intuitiveness lurk some deep philosophical and political questions about the nature of rationality, welfare and agency; the epistemics of regulation; and the fine line between 'nudges' and manipulation. Thus, the new paternalism has since been the subject of much fierce debate. It is to some of these debates that the essays comprising this volume contribute, albeit at times indirectly, through a discussion of the ideas of two giants in the history of economics and philosophy: Adam Smith and David Hume.

---

[2] A 401(k) account is a tax-advantaged, employer-sponsored retirement savings account for workers in the US.

My own background is in eighteenth-century political economy and moral philosophy. I am not a specialist in behavioural economics. Yet in following some of the debates surrounding behavioural welfare economics from a distance over the past few years, I have been struck by the extent to which Smith's and Hume's ideas might be recruited to support certain lines of criticism of the new paternalism. That Smith's and Hume's formulations dovetail with existing criticisms is perhaps natural enough – Smith and Hume are seminal figures in the classical liberal tradition in political economy in which many critics of the new paternalism work (e.g. Rizzo and Whitman 2020; Delmotte and Dold 2022; Sugden 2018; Dold 2018; see also Smith and Wilson 2019). But what is especially interesting is that one finds insights in Smith and Hume about human behaviour that resonate with the findings of contemporary behavioural economists and psychologists. Smith and Hume indicated a keen awareness of, for instance, our asymmetric valuation of gains and losses, the time-inconsistency of our preferences and the role of situational framing (see, for example, Palacious-Huerta 2003; Ashraf et al. 2005; Sugden 2006; Khalil 2010; Paganelli 2011). Observing such resonances, Richard Thaler, in his presidential address to the American Economic Association, said (Thaler 2016: 1578):

> George Stigler was fond of saying that there was nothing new in economics, as it had all been said by Adam Smith. It turns out that was true for behavioral economics as well.

More recently Robert Sugden (2021) claimed along similar lines that 'if behavioral economists were to look for a patron philosopher, Hume would be the obvious candidate.'

Smith and Hume are therefore interesting in the present context because we see remarkable points of convergence between their descriptive accounts of human action and those in modern behavioural science, but at the same time we find intellectual resources for different normative conclusions and recommendations than those of the new paternalism. These different conclusions derive, I think, partly from different operative notions of rationality and welfare, as well as from some scepticism of aspects of the political process on Smith's and Hume's part. The material here mostly deals with the former (rationality and welfare), and in the chapters I develop Smithian and Humean perspectives on these that complement existing perspectives critical of the new paternalism.

Smith and Hume wrote three hundred years ago in a different place and time; we must take care when drawing their ideas into present debates. But their ideas nonetheless can inform and inspire current discourses by providing new or at least forgotten perspectives and complementing new discoveries. We do well to, as Edmund Burke said, '[avail ourselves] of the general bank and capital of nations, and of ages' (Burke 1999: 182) and bring the wisdom of the past to bear on problems of the present.

Chapters 2–4 were written on separate occasions, and they may be read as standalone pieces. Chapter 1 provides a very broad historical sketch of the development of behavioural economics and the new paternalism, intended for the non-specialist; it also introduces some of the criticisms of the new paternalism that have been raised and provides an overview of the subsequent chapters in the volume. At times, the chapters (especially 3 and 4) veer into the territory of intellectual history and leave the explicit context of behavioural economics and paternalism behind. My hope, however, is that together they offer perspectives on some of the underlying philosophical issues that have been brought forth by the behavioural turn and, furthermore, contribute to our appreciation of the sophistication and continued value of the thought of two eighteenth-century Scotsmen.

Chapter 2 was previously published by the *Journal of Economic Methodology* (Matson 2022). Chapter 3 appeared in a special issue of the *Journal of Economic Behavior and Organization* (Matson 2021c), which I had the privilege of coediting with Mario Rizzo. Chapter 4, which I co-authored with Malte Dold (Matson and Dold 2021), appeared in a special issue of the *Review of Behavioral Economics* on Mario Rizzo and Glen Whitman's 2020 book, *Escaping Paternalism: Rationality, Behavioral Economics, and Public Policy*. The essays are reproduced from the published versions with only minor editing throughout, and I thank the journals for granting permission to reprint the material.

Much of the inspiration behind these essays comes from the work of Mario Rizzo and Glen Whitman. I spent two years as a postdoctoral fellow under Mario at NYU from 2018 to 2020; he encouraged me to consider the relevance of my interest in intellectual history for contemporary issues in behavioural economics. Thanks also to my friend and colleague Malte Dold (co-author of chapter 4) for his inspiring work on the philosophy of behavioural economics and for his constructive feedback on chapter 2. Dan Klein generously read and commented on the entire manuscript. Finally, a special word of thanks to James Forder at the IEA for inviting me to write a blogpost on Adam Smith and paternalism in October 2021. Without James's initiative, I never would have thought to publish these essays together as a collection.

# 1 ECONOMICS, PSYCHOLOGY AND THE NEW PATERNALISM

In this chapter, I provide a broad historical sketch of behavioural economics and the rise of the new paternalism. I then survey several of the main threads of recent criticism of the new paternalism and summarise the main themes of chapters 2–4 of this volume.

## The rise of behavioural economics

In his *Principles of Economics*, first published in 1890, Alfred Marshall defined economics as 'a study of mankind in the ordinary business of life; it examines that part of individual and social action which is most closely connected with the attainment and with the use of the material requisites of well-being' (Marshall 1920: 1). In place of the word 'action' we could substitute 'behaviour'. If that's correct, the phrase 'behavioural economics' appears to be a 'confusing pleonasm' (Heukelom 2014: 2). If economics is about behaviour relating to the ordinary business of life, isn't economics 'behavioural' by definition?

To understand the 'behavioural' element in behavioural economics, it helps to have a sense of the historical dynamics between economics and psychology.[1] Early writers in economics worked upstream of the extended intellectual division of labour that we now take for granted. In Britain, Josiah Tucker, David Hume, Adam Smith and William Paley moved easily between psychology, economics, ethics, politics – and even theology – all within a broad conception of 'moral philosophy'.

In the eighteenth and nineteenth centuries, British thinkers came to pay increased attention to the concept of usefulness, or 'utility'. In 1725 Francis Hutcheson advanced an understanding of right behaviour as that which 'procures the greatest Happiness for the greatest numbers' (Hutcheson 2008: 125). In his *Enquiry Concerning the Principles of Morals*, David Hume (1998) argued that we approve of the social virtues (especially justice) principally based on their utility – their ability to enable pleasurable and agreeable ends. Although his ethics somewhat downplay considerations of utility, Adam Smith argued in *The Theory of Moral Sentiments* that we ought to heed the 'system of behavior which tends to promote the happiness either of the individual or of the society' (Smith 1982: 326). This aspect of his ethics serves as one bridge to *The Wealth of Nations*. Political economy emerged to inform legislators on how to serve the happiness of society. It was originally, in large part, a science of statecraft.

The classical economists such as Smith, Ricardo and Mill had largely built their theories around general

---

[1] For a full-length treatment of this topic, on which I rely at various points in this chapter, see Heukelom (2014).

characterisations or stylised principles of human action (Heukelom 2014: ch. 2). Smith, for example, posited a propensity to truck, barter and exchange and a natural desire to better one's condition. Subsequent generations of economists attempted to refine such principles, reconsidering their source, scope and correspondence with other scientific findings, to better understand the logic of social interaction and human behaviour.

In refining the classical economist's stylised principles, thinkers such as Jeremy Bentham and William Stanley Jevons recast the concept of utility from a notion of social usefulness into ideas of subjective benefits and costs themselves, on the understanding that individuals seek the pleasure of gain and avoid the loss of pain. In the hands of Bentham and Jevons, and then Francis Edgeworth, 'utility' involved forays into hedonic psychology. Jevons contended that 'a true theory of economy can only be attained by going back to the great spirit of human action, the feelings of pleasure and pain,' which are constitutive of utility (quoted in Vaggi and Groenewegen 2003: 204). Edgeworth, now known principally for his diagrammatic analysis of two-person exchange (the 'Edgeworth Box'), took inspiration from the burgeoning field of psychophysics in Germany associated with the work of Ernst Weber and G. T. Fechner. Weber's experiments, popularised by Fechner, attempted to discover connections between an individual's sensory perception and physical stimulus (Colander 2007: 218–19). Building on such ideas, Edgeworth proposed a science of 'hedonimetry' for systematically measuring and then aggregating individuals' utilities. Hedonimetry was seen by Edgeworth as an important component of economics. Once an individual's experienced utilities are measured and understood, Edgeworth believed, a more precise science of choice could be formulated, and progress could be made towards formulating policies in service of enhancing human pleasure.

Scepticism about deploying hedonic psychology in economics came forth early in the twentieth century, for instance in the thought of Phillip Wicksteed. Although a great admirer of Jevons, Wicksteed looked to advance the marginal-utility approach to price theory independent of particular psychologies of utility (Drakopoulus 2011). The American economist Irving Fisher similarly opposed psychologising economics. 'This foisting of Psychology on Economics,' he wrote, 'seems to me inappropriate and vicious' (Fisher 1892: 5). For Fisher, the economist ought not to concern himself with the psychological foundations of utility but rather infer utility from observed choice on the basis of a simple 'psychoeconomic postulate: Each individual acts as he desires' (quoted in Colander 2007: 220). This approach, he thought, would improve the explanatory abilities of economics since it provided a readily measured conception of utility: choice itself (Colander 2007: 219).

Aspects of Fisher's approach anticipate the approach to economics that arose after World War II. That approach was in part a reaction against hedonic psychology, which was thought to limit the generality and explanatory power of economic theory. Paul Samuelson wrote of 'the theory of consumer's choice [marching] steadily towards greater generality, sloughing off ... unnecessarily restrictive conditions' like 'the assumption of the measurability of utility in a cardinal sense' (Samuelson 1938: 61). A new approach emerged, attempting to build on generalisable postulates about choice free from psychological baggage. This approach is now often glossed over as 'neoclassical economics'.

Neoclassical economics took inspiration from several currents of thought. Philosophically, it aspired (and still aspires, in some cases) to be 'mindless economics' (Gul and Pesendorfer 2010). This aspiration reflected the rise of behaviourism and logical positivism. Behaviourism holds that hypotheses about mental states must be confirmed in terms of observed behaviour (see Sellars 1963: 22). Logical positivism centres on the propositions that knowledge is either by definition or observed experience, and that knowledge advances through a process of refuting or failing to refute falsifiable propositions. In keeping with these ideas, neoclassical economists came to view the mind as a sort of black box about which we can draw inferences and develop and test hypotheses only from observed behaviours.

In addition to behaviourism and positivism, neoclassical economics relied on new axiomatic approaches to probabilistic decision-making, that is, decision-making in situations of risk. Axiomatic decision theory was pioneered by John von Neumann and Oskar Morgenstern in 1944 in their book *Theory of Games and Economic Behavior*. Von Neumann and Morgenstern attempted 'to find the mathematically complete principles which define "rational behavior" for the participants in a social economy, and to derive from them the general characteristics of that behavior' (von Neumann and Morgenstern 2004: 31). Drawing from traditional assumptions made by economists, they characterised 'rational behavior' as that which 'obtain[s] a maximum of utility or satisfaction' on the part of a consumer and 'a maximum of profits' on the part of an entrepreneur (von Neumann and Morgenstern 2004: 8; see discussion in Heukelom 2014: ch. 2).

Von Neumann and Morgenstern had no wish to measure individuals' utility directly, contrary to Jevons, Edgeworth and Fisher. But discriminating in a model between rational and irrational decision-making requires a rank-ordering of outcomes; rank-ordering requires assigning preferences ordinal values. If I like chocolate more than vanilla, chocolate can be represented with '2' and vanilla with '1'. The assigning of ordinal values, in turn, calls forth logical axioms about preference relations. Two key axioms are completeness and transitivity: a person's preferences must be complete (for any two preferences A and B, either $A > B$, $A < B$, or $A = B$) and transitive (if $A > B$, and $B > C$, then $A > C$). The full set of axioms implied by a numerical utility scale defines von Neumann and Morgenstern's formal conception of rationality. That concept of rationality has since taken hold among many economists, both neoclassical and, somewhat ironically, behavioural.

In the late 1940s and into the 1950s, economists and psychologists debated the significance of von Neumann and Morgenstern's theory (Heukelom 2014: ch. 3). Was the axiomatic definition of rationality a prescription for how rational people *ought* to behave? Was it a description of human behaviour? Was it a falsifiable theory? Figures such as Paul Samuelson, William Baumol, Milton Friedman, Leonard Savage and Maurice Allais debated the issue.

Friedman's perspective appears in the classic statement of his economic philosophy, 'The Methodology of Positive Economics' (Friedman 1953). That statement is a central articulation of the philosophical outlook of neoclassical economics. Drawing on positivist ideas about science, Friedman maintained that the credibility of a theory lies in its ability to predict. Whether human beings are *actually* rational in the axiomatic sense is irrelevant; what matters is whether the assumption that they are helps us predict their behaviour. And, as Friedman argues, it does. It might be the case that the consumer is not consciously equalising her marginal rates of substitution. Yet the assumption that she is attempting to do so aligns well with her behaviour, at least in some important instances.

But what happens when the theory doesn't align with observed behaviour? Is the theory to be discarded? Such questions cast light on the rise of behavioural economics and the road by which psychology has, once again, come into closer contact with economic theory.

In the 1950s, William Baumol and Paul Samuelson challenged von Neumann and Morgenstern's theory on the grounds that it inadequately captured the character of individuals' risk aversion (e.g. Baumol 1951; discussion in Heukelom 2014: ch. 3). A similar challenge was later levelled by the French economist Maurice Allais. Allais's challenge took the form of a paradox. Here is the paradox presented in a somewhat simplified form recently by the psychologist Daniel Kahneman in his popular book *Thinking, Fast and Slow* (2011: 313):

> In problems A and B, which would you choose?
> - 61% chance to win $520,000 OR 63% chance to win $500,000
> - 98% chance to win $520,000 OR 100% chance to win $500,000
>
> If you are like most other people, you preferred the left-hand option in problem A and you preferred the right-hand option in problem B.

This is a paradox because selecting the left-hand option in A and the right-hand option in B is logically inconsistent. The chance to win an extra $20,000 in A seems well worth the slightly lower overall probability of winning (61 per cent instead of 63 per cent); in B, for some reason, winning an additional $20,000 is not worth the same decrease in winning odds (98 per cent instead of 100 per cent) for most people. For some reason, 'the 2% difference between a 100% and a 98% chance to win in problem B is vastly more impressive than the same difference between 63% and 61% in problem A' (Kahneman 2011: 314).

Allais presented this paradox (in a different form) in 1952 to Leonard Savage, a defender of von Neumann and Morgenstern's approach. After carefully considering the paradox, Savage told Allais, effectively, that he too would choose left in A and right in B, although he knew it to be logically inconsistent. He admitted to Allais that his choice was 'irrational' but he still thought the von Neumann and

Morgenstern approach to be 'good characterizations of rational behavior' that usefully depict and predict human behaviour (Heukelom 2014: 56). A problem for Savage's contention began to emerge out of the growing literature in cognitive psychology, especially starting in the 1970s.

Cognitive psychology, against behaviourism, aimed to 'open the mind's black box and to investigate how its different constituents ... interact to produce behavior' (Heukelom 2014: 97). A group of cognitive psychologists, spearheaded by Daniel Kahneman and Amos Tversky, aimed to bring such research methods to bear on economics. Their findings illustrated that individuals' behaviour often deviates from the standards of neoclassical decision theory. Those deviations are not random but systematic; they stem predictably from general aspects of human psychology.

Kahneman and Tversky's research programme in the 1970s led to a reformulation of von Neumann and Morgenstern's axiomatic decision theory, labelled 'prospect theory' and elaborated in a 1979 article in the journal *Econometrica*. Prospect theory builds on a body of evidence suggesting that the expected utility of an outcome depends on one's anchor or point of reference. When faced with potential losses, individuals tend to be more risk-averse than when faced with potential gains. The expected utility of winning $20 is outweighed by the expected disutility of losing the $20 after it is won. Prospect theory has many implications for consumer theory, one being that consumers' willingness to pay for an item might differ from the price they are willing to accept for the same item. Exchange asymmetries along these lines were documented in a famous experiment by Kahneman et al. (1991).

Related lines of work in economics, starting as early as R. H. Strotz (1956), pointed to the inability of classical decision theory to explain weakness of will, preference reversals and the strategies that we commonly employ to overcome myopia. Healthier eating, more exercise and higher rates of savings are things that we often find ourselves desiring, but they are difficult for us to realise in practice. We are sometimes willing to impose future costs on ourselves for those ends. Thomas Schelling (1980) wrote eloquently (although in somewhat of a different mode) along similar lines about our 'intimate contest for self-command'. It was believed that exploring our mental equipment could offer insight into the logic of these decisions and enhance the explanations of consumer choice offered by neoclassical economics. Traditional models that assume agents to exponentially discount expected utility have, for instance, on occasion been replaced by models featuring hyperbolic discount rates to accommodate observed anomalies such as preference reversals (Laibson 1997).

In the 1990s and 2000s the incorporation of cognitive psychology and neuroscience into the neoclassical framework consolidated into the research programme that we now call 'behavioural economics'. Many behavioural economists see their project simply as an extension of and improvement from within the neoclassical project. Along these lines, Matthew Rabin contended that behavioural economics 'does not abandon the correct insights of neoclassical economics, but supplements these insights with the insights to be had from realistic new assumptions' (Rabin 2002: 658–59). In the words of the prominent behavioural economists Colin Camerer and George Loewenstein (2003: 3), 'behavioral economics increase the explanatory power of economics by providing it with more realistic psychological foundations'. Behavioural economics has, in the past twenty years, grown in influence and made inroads into the economics profession. Echoing Milton Friedman's comments on the methodological influence of John Maynard Keynes, Erik Angner (2019) goes so far as to contend that 'we're all behavioral economists now.' That is, integrating insights from behavioural sciences and admitting the descriptive shortcomings of aspects of classical decision theory has become increasingly prevalent in mainstream economic research.

## The new paternalism: origins and criticism

In the early days behavioural economics was not associated with an approach to public policy. In the past twenty years, however, some behavioural economists and psychologists have developed distinctive approaches to politics. Perhaps the earliest – and certainly the most famous – articulations of an approach occurred in 2003 in two papers: 'Regulation for Conservatives' (Camerer et al. 2003) and 'Libertarian Paternalism' (Sunstein and Thaler 2003a). These papers gave rise, along with related literature, to new strategies for policy – new paternalist strategies. Such strategies, popularised especially by Richard Thaler and Cass Sunstein's (2009) *Nudge*, have gained traction around the world over the last fifteen years. The new paternalism inspired the development of devoted behavioural science units in the US federal government under Barack Obama and in the UK government under David Cameron (Halpern 2015).

The new paternalism implicitly revolves around notions of decision-making failure. There is a long history of market failure theories in economics. Those theories hold that unregulated markets fail to bring about an efficient distribution of goods and services. Everyone might make the right decision for himself, but these decisions don't aggregate into the proper decision for the population. The classic examples of market failure involve externalities such as pollution and public goods. Decision-making failure theories go beyond market failure theories, maintaining that individuals make decisions that, whether or not they harm the population, harm individuals by their own subjective standards.

The proposition that we sometimes make wrong decisions from our own perspective is intuitive; the new paternalism brings research from cognitive psychology and neuroscience to bear on the intuition. The new paternalists argue that we predictably act against our true desires because of various elements of our psychology. We would like to select healthy snack options, but sometimes the salient positioning of a candy bar, combined with our hunger, leads us to do otherwise (Read and van Leeuwen 1998). Decision-making failures are exacerbated by our cognitive limitations and errors in reasoning. Complex situations can be overwhelming (Beshears et al. 2008: 1788–89) and can lead us, for example, to opt for poorly understood default options in retirement contributions (O'Donoghue and Rabin 1999; Iyengar et al. 2004) or education options for our children (Thaler and Sunstein 2009: 201–8). Even in instances when we have a good sense of what we want, along with the willpower to realise our wants, we sometimes make calculation or 'characterization' mistakes (Bernheim 2016: 48), such as in assessing the value of financial assets (Ambuehl et al. 2022).

In recognition of our decision-making failures, the new paternalism looks to change aspects of our choice environments – i.e. the physical and ideational contexts of choices – such that those environments cooperate with our psychology and help us to do what we really want to do. This effort at influencing choice by altering our decision-making environments is often called 'choice architecture'. A famous example comes from the opening pages of Thaler and Sunstein (2009), where they discuss a cafeteria manager who chooses to prominently display healthy items and move desserts to the background. This manager doesn't prevent individuals from selecting desserts, but by not displaying them prominently, she increases (it is claimed) the likelihood that consumers will select healthy items. On the assumption that those healthy items are what consumers really want to choose, the cafeteria manager is helping individuals achieve their own goals. Other examples of choice architecture involve various degrees of coercion: taxes on alcohol, tobacco and sugar to decrease the present allure of addictive activities (O'Donoghue and Rabin 2003); the placing of ghastly images on products such as cigarettes to communicate consumption narratives; the requiring of specific default options for labour contracts and retirement contributions (Sunstein and Thaler 2003b: 1175–78); and even the outright banning of harmful but highly attractive products such as trans fats (Conly 2013). Within the new paternalist paradigm, these policy initiatives aim to 'influence choices in a way that will make choosers better off as judged by themselves' (Thaler and Sunstein 2009: 5), and they thus differ from classical paternalism.

To suppose that you can make a person better off as judged by himself, as the new paternalists have claimed, requires a method of identifying situations in which a person is not acting in his best interest. In practice, many of the new paternalists over the past several decades have fallen back on a neoclassical conception of rationality as an error-identification strategy (Infante et al. 2016; Rizzo 2017). Neoclassical rationality offers an attractive baseline, for it offers a seemingly clear, value-neutral (from the evaluator's perspective) litmus test of error: if a person is behaving inconsistently – i.e. expressing a preference for X over Y but choosing Y, or expressing a preference for X but evident calculation errors in attempting to achieve X – she must be in error. If one expresses a preference for exercise over sleep but continues to sleep through her alarms in the morning, one might reasonably conclude that helping her wake up in the morning will make her better off.

Two common criticisms of such an approach are: (1) rationality is broader than its neoclassical conception and (2) welfare often involves a dynamic component – it is not simply about satisfying a static set of preferences. On the first: in their pioneering 1944 work, von Neumann and Morgenstern did not intend to provide a comprehensive definition of human rationality. They worked out a novel theory of choice under uncertainty, and that theory required mathematical assumptions for tractability. 'They did not posit [their] axioms as a unique definition of rationality, nor did they imbue them with normative significance' (Rizzo and Whitman 2020: 53). The neoclassical conception of rationality, in other words, might be useful for modelling purposes, but it should not be viewed as a realistic description of how people act or a recommendation as to how they should. In the common course of life, inconsistency in choice need not be viewed as pathological – many observed sets of behaviours purported to be inconsistent can, with proper attention to context, be illuminated as processes of learning in a complex environment. Rationality is more of a dynamic process of adaptation than a state of affairs (cf. Smith 2003; Rescher 1987; Rizzo and Whitman 2018); change and inconsistency are often essential to our growth and self-understanding and our efforts to carve out a sense of meaning and calling in life.

On the second point, a challenge to new paternalism emerges as we consider welfare not simply as a matter of satisfying existing preferences but in dynamic terms of self-improvement and transformation. What if what people really want is not simply to conform to a predetermined mould of health, wealth and happiness but to improve themselves? What if an important part of our flourishing as human beings lies in a sense of doing and progressing towards what is right and beautiful? The economist Frank

Knight claimed along these lines that what 'the common sense individual wants is not satisfaction for the wants which he has, but more and better wants' (Knight 1922: 458). Hume, as elaborated in chapter 3, had a similar perspective, which lay at the heart of his positive evaluation of a free, commercial society. People desire to improve their conditions, not just materially but morally and aesthetically. Such improvements require opportunity and cannot be realised without some degree of experimentation and even error. If Knight and Hume are correct – and I think they are (cf. Dold and Rizzo 2021) – economists and social scientists interested in helping individuals become better off must recalibrate away from the new paternalism. A better approach to helping people is to tend to the broad institutional and cultural contexts in which preferences are developed (on this general point, see Dold and Schubert 2018; Schubert 2015). We can encourage open discourse about our limitations and psychological quirks and how they should figure into our decision-making processes. We can focus on cultivating a vibrant, free society in which people have opportunities to learn and develop their capacities through education, meaningful vocation and voluntary association.

Together, the above points about rationality and the nature of welfare suggest that identifying behavioural errors and designing policy to make individuals better off as judged by their own standards is much more difficult than it seems – perhaps it is impossible (cf. Thoma 2021; Cartwright and Hight 2019). This in turn would imply that the new paternalism might not actually be so different from classical paternalism. That is, in pursuing new paternalist-style policies, regulators, policymakers and choice architects are not simply helping individuals do what the individuals themselves want, for that is too difficult; they are simply attempting to make individuals do something that they (the regulators) believe will improve their lives, irrespective of the individuals' own consent. It might be the case that, in select instances, policies of this sort are ethically permissible and politically desirable (Hausman 2018). Using public policy to decrease obesity or alcoholism, for example, might be a good thing – especially when the healthcare costs of obesity or liver failure are borne by the tax-paying population (assuming a world of government-provided healthcare). Behavioural research can of course be useful on these fronts. But at this point we simply have something close to classical paternalism, not new paternalism, and the policy proposals need to be justified as such.

## A bridge from the eighteenth century

The subsequent chapters in this book approach the above issues of rationality and welfare through some discussion of the ideas of Adam Smith and David Hume. Chapter 2, 'Our dynamic being within: a Smithian critique of the new paternalism', elaborates Smith's ideas of practical reason or deliberation as a learning process that involves reflecting on disjointed perspectives. Smith's ideas are drawn on to illustrate why inconsistency (e.g. voicing a preference for fruit but selecting cake) does not necessarily indicate error.

Consistency might be an ideal towards which we strive, as we attempt to refine our desires and act accordingly; but it is, in and of itself, 'not a fundamental prerequisite for rationality' (Rescher 1987: 303). Understanding the potential reasonableness of inconsistency complicates the error-identification strategy of the new paternalists.

Chapter 2 also draws on Smith to comment on the dynamic aspect of human welfare. Smith understands a significant part of our well-being to reside not simply in the satisfaction of the right desires but in pursuing and refining our desires. The desire to better our condition – a central principle in Smith's economics – includes not just the desire to improve our material conditions but the desire to improve our character, preferences and tastes. This point is advanced by treating Smith's idea of self-judgement in connection with his theory of the impartial spectator. Smith poeticises the deliberative nature of rationality as a conversation between our acting self and our inner being, personified as the conscience. We want the sympathy of our conscience, but the desires of our conscience unfold in various ways across different contexts as we encounter novel choice situations. The dynamic aspect of well-being appears when we consider that the conscience has a conscience – the highest impartial spectator, or The Impartial Spectator. Even as our conscience deliberates with our acting self about the proper course of action, he deliberates with The Impartial Spectator over *his* proper course of judgement, which he then attempts to pass on to the acting self. This metaphorical conception of choice that we can draw from Smith points towards the upward vitality of the human spirit and the longing for improvement. It is a very different concept of well-being than that featured in the new paternalist discourse – and in economics generally. It implies a real challenge for those who would nudge us to make us better off, as judged by ourselves. How can someone nudge us into a course of action that will make us better off by our own standards if we ourselves are unsure what those standards are? Again, this sort of dilemma pushes new paternalism back into the same position as old paternalism – imposing a conception of good conduct on an individual in the belief that she will subsequently recognise it as beneficial, even though it lies outside of her current set of desires.

Chapter 3, 'Satisfaction in action: Hume's endogenous theory of preferences and the virtues of commerce', offers further reflections on dynamic aspects of welfare. Studies indicate that preferences in some cases do not precede choice but are elicited in the moment of choice (Lichtenstein and Slovic 2006). When going to a restaurant, we sometimes have a well-formed sense of what we'd like but other times we make in-time decisions when the server is at the table. In economic jargon, preferences in such instances can be said to be 'endogenous' (as opposed to 'exogenous', or 'existing outside of') to the choice situation. The endogeneity of preferences explains advertising practices and marketing schemes. The notion of preference endogeneity has been a cause for concern among some commentators. John Kenneth Galbraith, for example, criticised the free market for perpetuating artificial and unhealthy desires through advertising and marketing. In the early twentieth century, Thorstein Veblen identified conspicuous consumption ('keeping up with the Joneses') as a vicious aspect of modern commerce. Hume, like Galbraith, Veblen and a host of contemporary behavioural economists and scientists, understands preferences to be endogenous: what we want is a function of social influences that operate both through general cultural context and the social framing of particular choices. Yet Hume maintains an ardent enthusiasm about the moral and cultural effects of the market. This is partly because he conceives of human happiness in dynamic terms and believes that commercial society affords unparalleled opportunities for individuals to transform themselves and pursue and refine their desires. As one Hume scholar put it, 'economic behavior [for Hume] involves not merely a desire for want-gratification but further reflects a desire to *have* and *pursue* wants' (Rotwein 2009: xlvii).

Chapter 4, co-authored with Malte Dold, was written as a review essay of Mario Rizzo and Glen Whitman's (2020) important book, *Escaping Paternalism*. Our essay further elaborates Hume's ideas about human happiness and connects those ideas with reflections on the role of the philosopher – or behavioural scientist – in society. The main theme is that there are different conceivable paths to the good life. These paths are at times incommensurable and cannot be resolved by the philosopher or the economist. The political implication of this perspective is that we should leave deliberations about the higher things in life to individuals and voluntary associations, at least to a large extent.

The behavioural economist should not view herself as one possessed of privileged knowledge about the good life, but she should adopt the posture of an advisor offering information and friendly advice. People should feel full confidence in their freedom to decline the offer. Insofar as behavioural scientists believe that individuals are making errors, they ought to inform the individuals directly, in a non-coercive fashion, rather than imposing their will or pulling strings behind the scenes.

Smith and Hume developed their ideas in a different social and historical context that is in some ways quite distant from today. It is of course anachronistic to draw from their writings for present purposes – the historical Adam Smith and David Hume obviously had nothing to say about behavioural economics or the new paternalism as such. But their philosophical formulations and insights into human nature are, nonetheless, of continued relevance, for in a fundamental sense human nature does not change. 'Would you know the sentiments, inclinations, and course of life of the Greeks and Romans? Study well the temper and actions of the French and English,' Hume wrote. 'You cannot be much mistaken in transferring to the former *most* of the observations which you have made with regard to the latter' (Hume 2000: 64).

The insights generated from the behavioural turn in the social sciences have opened new lines of thinking on human action and created different possibilities for policymaking. We can draw on the wisdom of the past, such as that found across the writings of Hume and Smith – men who appreciated the rich social and psychological complexity of human action – as we develop responses to contemporary developments. We can, as James Buchanan wrote, 'exploit "Adam Smith" [and also David Hume], metaphorically, by imputing to him a vision that ... becomes scientifically coherent and normatively satisfying,' a vision that can be taken as a logical extension or development of his ideas (Buchanan 2008: 21). The vision that emerges in the following essays from this exercise welcomes the many interesting findings of behavioural science, but it holds that these do not require or warrant a new paternalistic regime. Our two Scots appreciated some of the peculiarities of choice that are today noted by behavioural scientists, peculiarities that lead us to behave in ways that contradict the axioms of classical expected utility theory. But Smith and Hume did not, evidently, envision a need for widespread government paternalism or a nanny state. One could argue that this was simply because new paternalist–style policies were not then a viable policy option. One could argue that if they had sufficiently appreciated the beneficial potentials of the regulation of choice architecture, they would have supported such efforts. Perhaps. On the other hand, we might imagine them dissenting from paternalist-style proposals based on their ideas about welfare, rationality and the epistemic limits and slippery slopes of regulation, and it is along these lines and in this spirit that I offer these essays.

## 2 OUR DYNAMIC BEING WITHIN: SMITHIAN CHALLENGES TO THE NEW PATERNALISM

In this chapter I use aspects of the analytical framework of Adam Smith's *The Theory of Moral Sentiments* (TMS) to elucidate critiques about the new paternalism relating to the context dependence of preferences[1] and the dynamic aspects of welfare.[2] These imply that there is nothing inherently unreasonable about inconsistent behaviour and

---

1 In twentieth-century economics, the prominent interpretation of the concept of preference derived from behaviourism. Preferences, on the behaviourist interpretation, have no reference to mental phenomena; preferences are simply revealed in the act of choice (Samuelson 1938; Gul and Pesendorfer 2010). My use of 'preference' here, however, follows a mentalist interpretation – the referents of 'preferences' are comparative desires that cause agents to act to realise those desires (see discussion in Vredenburgh 2021: 69).

2 The only other paper I know that engages with the new paternalism on Smithian grounds is Otteson (2018), which brings Smith into conversation with Thaler and Sunstein's 'libertarian paternalism.' Otteson says that from a Smithian perspective, 'the entire range of nudges' in Thaler and Sunstein might be justified 'as areas in which private enterprise cannot or at least does not help society meet optimal results' (Otteson 2018: 250). It is important to note that the new paternalism, however, is mainly motivated by notions of decision-making failure, rather than market failure. My argument here is that a Smithian perspective offers reasons for scepticism about decision-making failure narratives and evidence, thus challenging a key premise of the new paternalism.

that we should think about welfare as more than preference satisfaction. This creates epistemic and practical obstacles for the new paternalism and suggests new directions for behavioural economists interested in welfare.

## Setting the stage

Behavioural welfare economists employ various methods. But they operate within a similar framework. Drawing on research in neuroscience and psychology, the framework assumes that we systematically fail to behave rationally. These observations imply, against traditional welfare economics, that there is at best a loose correspondence between revealed preferences and welfare. On this view, welfare analysis – i.e. the study of how various institutional arrangements and policy changes impact individuals' well-being[3] – requires one to differentiate between welfare-improving and welfare-diminishing choices. Our choices may be said to be welfare-improving only if they satisfy the right preferences.[4] In much of behavioural welfare economics, right or true preferences are preferences that have been purified from various psychological distortions and calculation errors (Hausman 2012: 86) and can

---

[3] Welfare and well-being are not necessarily synonymous, but they appear normally to be used in interchangeable ways in behavioural welfare economics. See, for instance, the usage of the terms in Sunstein (2020). See also the three propositions of Bernheim's (2016, 33) 'choice-oriented welfare framework,' which centre on the concept of well-being.

[4] For a wide-ranging discussion on the distinction between present desires and desires 'that one knows one would [have] were one fully informed and rational', see Railton (1986: 14).

therefore be 'integrated' into a complete, logical account of choice (Sugden 2018: 7). Once welfare-relevant preferences have been distinguished, institutions and public policies can be designed to alter our decision-making environment (choice architecture) such that it cooperates with our psychology and helps us do what we in fact would like to do.

The project of the new paternalism, in other words, is 'to influence choices in a way that will make choosers better off *as judged by themselves*' (Thaler and Sunstein 2009: 5; italics in original). 'Paternalism' may be defined here in terms of its aims 'to benefit people by getting them to make choices that are good for themselves' and by the fact that 'choosers would agree with this evaluation of their choice' (Hausman and Welch 2010: 126). This definition of paternalism is problematic in that it does not sufficiently differentiate between interventions that limit freedom of choice and interventions that do not (Hausman and Welch 2010: 126–29; see also Klein 2004).[5] But for present purposes, we can set those concerns aside and engage with problems in methodology and philosophy of the new paternalism on its own terms.

How can new paternalists identify choices that people will judge as making themselves better off? This is the critical problem for the new paternalist project, and different methods appear to solve it.[6] A prominent method – which

---

5 Sunstein and Thaler (2003b: 1185), for example, describe the coerciveness of new paternalist interventions as a continuum.

6 Some methods rely on direct measurements of reported subjective utility and well-being (see contributions to Kahneman et al. 1999; for critical discussion, see Bernheim 2016). Others seem to draw on folk psychologies

is a main target of my criticism here – is to distinguish welfare-relevant or normative preferences from revealed preferences by virtue of their conformity to axioms of rational choice theory (e.g. Bleichrodt et al. 2001; Kőszegi and Rabin 2007; Salant and Rubinstein 2008; Beshears et al. 2008; Thaler and Sunstein 2009; Bernheim and Rangel 2007).[7] If revealed preferences violate the axioms of rational choice, they can be said to evince irrationality; they can be said to be welfare-diminishing.

The relevant axioms of choice are completeness and transitivity, from which derive two corollaries. The completeness axiom holds that 'for any two objects $(x, y)$ in the set of alternatives (X) we must have $x R y$ or $y R x$ or both', where R means 'is ranked at least as highly as' (Rizzo and Whitman 2020: 43). The transitivity axiom holds that for all $x, y, z$ in X, if $x R y$ and $y R z$, then $x R z$ (ibid.). The two corollaries are the Independence of Irrelevant Alternatives (IIA) and Framing Invariance. The IIA axiom maintains that if $x R y$ when $z$ is available, then $x R y$ when $z$ is not available (and vice versa). The Framing Invariance axiom holds that all 'preference relations are entirely unaffected by the manner in which alternatives are described' (ibid.). Put together, these four axioms provide an account of rational choice as a matter of consistency, across contexts and over time (Rizzo and Whitman 2020: 45; Berg 2014).

---

of well-being (see discussion in Hausman 2018). Some also consider facts about the world (for example, scientific findings concerning health and nutrition) in conjunction with individuals' expressed preferences (Sunstein 2020; Conly 2013).

7   For a discussion of 'debiased welfare analysis' see Thoma (2019).

## Smith on self-awareness and self-judgement

How exactly do Smith's ideas relate to such concepts and formulations? At first glance, it might appear that the objects of analysis of behavioural welfare economics and the new paternalism are incongruent with those of Smith's system in TMS. Behavioural welfare economics and the new paternalism deal mostly with mundane, self-regarding behaviour concerning health, wealth and happiness. TMS, on the other hand, appears to deal principally with rules of social interaction, conceptions of virtue, and ethics more generally. What do choices about diet, exercise, savings and health insurance have to do with social norms, ideas of virtue, and ethical sensibilities?

One answer is that irrespective of the context in which they were developed, Smith's formulations in TMS provide a useful way to conceptualise choice. A second point is that a central part of TMS is, in fact, about self-assessment and the process of self-approval. The full title of TMS since its fourth edition (1774), which has unfortunately been obscured, makes the importance of self-assessment clear: *The Theory of Moral Sentiments, or An Essay towards an Analysis of the Principles by which Men naturally judge concerning the Conduct and Character, first of their Neighbours, and afterwards of themselves*. Issues of self-assessment or self-judgement are closely connected with concerns of the new paternalism to make individuals better off by their own internal standards.[8]

---

8   In the course of developing ideas about self-assessment, moreover, Smith directly touches upon on issues of interest to new paternalists like savings and the self-approbation we feel on exercising frugality (Smith 1982: 215).

## Smithian self-judgement

To understand Smith's ideas about self-judgement, we must first tend to his ideas about self-awareness. The idea of self-awareness concerns the way we develop a sense of our person as opposed to other people. Self-awareness for Smith involves moral and aesthetic awareness as we experience second-order passions about our more immediate passions. Smith's notion of self-awareness is key to developing Smithian perspectives on choice, error and welfare.

Smith's perspective on the matter comes across in a thought experiment in TMS Part III (Smith 1982: 110–11):

> Were it possible that a human creature could grow up to manhood in some solitary place, without any communication with his own species, he could think no more of his own character, of the propriety or demerit of his own sentiments and conduct, of the beauty or deformity of his own mind, than of the beauty or deformity of his own face. All these are objects which he cannot easily see, which naturally he does not look at, and with regard to which he is provided with no mirror which can present them to his view. Bring him into society, and he is immediately provided with the mirror which he wanted before. It is placed in the countenance and behaviour of those he lives with, which always mark when they enter into it, and when they disapprove of his sentiments. [...] Bring him into society, and all his own passions will immediately become the causes of new passion.

The human creature in the wild, perhaps some imaginary being such as Tarzan, lacks the reflexive self-awareness characteristic of a human person. It is only by experiencing the company of others, listening to and interpreting their speech, discerning their facial cues and physical movements (Schliesser 2017: 54–55), that we become self-aware in any meaningful sense of that phrase. Tarzan's lack of self-awareness is a function of his social isolation and lack of language, which is the chief means by which human beings interact, persuade and develop in community.

Smith's thought experiment is, in a way, ridiculous. No human being could survive for any meaningful length of time outside of some social context. But the thought experiment usefully illustrates the social and rhetorical dimensions of our self-awareness. Our sense of our person derives from a tacit view of our person as consisting in multiple and sometimes disjointed perspectives. The point is apparent in Smith's mirror metaphor. That metaphor implies that we see ourselves – and are hence self-aware – as we see others seeing us. Or, as Charles Griswold puts it, 'we are aware of ourselves through being aware that others are aware of us' (Griswold 1999: 107; see also Choi 1990: 294). The gradual act of seeing others see us from infancy inculcates in us an aesthetic consciousness of our body and physical movements. We come to 'examine our persons limb by limb' (Smith 1982: 112). We proceed from aesthetic to moral awareness. Our appetites and other instinctual impulses become the causes of new passions, mediated by social vision and sympathetic imagination. We learn to command our passions with our higher passions for propriety, social approval and virtue.

Drawing as they do from our experience of others seeing us, both our aesthetic and moral awareness rely on a metaphorical division of our person into two persons: the acting person and the judging person (Smith 1982: 113). The inner or judging person is the conscience, whom Smith (1982: 113) personifies throughout TMS as 'the man within the breast' or 'the man within':

> When I endeavour to examine my own conduct, when I endeavour to pass sentence upon it, and either to approve or condemn it, it is evident, in all such cases, I divide myself, as it were, into two persons; and that I, the examiner and judge, represent a different character from that other I, the person whose conduct is examined into and judged of. The first is the spectator, whose sentiments with regard to my own conduct I endeavour to enter into, by placing myself in his situation, and by considering how it would appear to me, when seen from that particular point of view. The second is the agent, the person whom I properly call myself, and whose conduct, under the character of a spectator, I was endeavouring to form some opinion.

Smith's talk of dividing ourselves into multiple persons needn't be taken as an ontological claim. He isn't saying that we comprise two distinct agents. (Note, in fact, that this passage features not two but three beings: the acting person, the judging person, and the first person 'I'.)

What Smith is doing here is making a phenomenological point about how we experience ourselves; from that point he proffers a metaphor through which we can speak of preference, choice and error. We talk about our preferences metaphorically as if we comprised multiple persons because that metaphor accords with our intuitive self-understanding.[9]

## Self-approval and reasonable inconsistencies

Drawing on observations of our natural desire for self-approbation and internal tranquility (Smith 1982: 149; see discussion at Griswold 1999: 134), Smith advances his metaphor of self-awareness and judgement on the assumption that the 'man within' represents our deepest-to-date preferences. The 'man within' is the great 'tribunal' to whom our acting person, the personification of our lower-level and more immediate passions, is subject (Smith 1982: 130). We desire his approval and seek to command our behaviour

---

[9] The Smithian theme of self-judgement by artificially separating ourselves into multiple persons features in the behavioural economics literature going back at least to Ashraf et al. (2005). Bénabou and Tirole (2006) integrate self-image incentives – that is, the desire to keep one's actions, values and feelings in congruence – into their comprehensive model of 'prosocial' behaviour. Khalil (2010) deploys Smith's ideas about self-spectatorship and self-command to present a solution to commitment problems. The 'man within' calls us to steel ourselves into dynamic consistency, and he punishes us by withholding his approbation if we fall short. On this point, see also Palacious-Huerta (2003). Most recently, Serdarveric (2021) draws on Smith's claims on our desire for praiseworthiness to account for experimental anomalies, like choosing less money in a dictator game. What we want is, in part, to appear worthy in the eyes of our 'man within', irrespective of what the 'man without' might say (cf. Andreoni and Bernheim 2009).

to earn it. Such a position might appear congenial to some behavioural welfare economists. New paternalists might even rephrase their agenda to make individuals better off as judged by themselves in Smithian terms: to aim to make individuals better off as judged by their consciences. Attention to the details of Smith's account of conscience and self-judgement, however, shows that his vision of practical reason can be used to undercut rather than support the new paternalism.

Mario Rizzo and Glen Whitman (2020) have argued that new paternalists have improperly appropriated ideas of rational conduct from twentieth-century decision theory. The appropriation is improper because the axiomatic notion of rationality was developed for the sake of mathematical modelling; it wasn't intended by its progenitors as a standard of practical reason (Rizzo 2017; see also Berg and Gigerenzer 2010). When we move beyond a commitment to a formalized 'rationality for puppets' (Rizzo and Whitman 2020: 39), we see that violations of the axioms of completeness and transitivity (and their corollaries) need not be viewed as pathological. Attention to the contexts of choice may often reveal good reason for framing effects and menu-dependence. Even logically equivalent choice sets are not always informationally equivalent: apparent inconsistency may simply reflect agents responding to reasonable environmental cues and reference points (McKenzie 2004). With broader ideas about human rationality much of the impetus behind new paternalist policies falls away. Smith's ideas about the dialogical nature of self-judgement reinforce such critiques.

In many instances our preferences emerge in the process of making choices. We sometimes lack well-formed ideas about our interests apart from the concrete act of choice (Lichtenstein and Slovic 2006; Loomes et al. 2010). Occasionally it appears that elements of our decision context influence our choices in ways that they should not. Assuming we have a preference for healthy food or junk food, the time of day, intuitively, should be irrelevant to our active choice between the two; but, of course, it has an effect (Read and van Leeuwen 1998). New paternalists often jump from observations of context-induced reversals in revealed preference to conclusions of irrationality and error. It might very well be the case that framing effects, for example, sometimes lead us to err. The *direction* of error, however, is not immediately clear, which raises difficulties for efforts in choice architecture: which of a pair of inconsistent revealed preferences should we privilege (Rizzo and Whitman 2007: 419–20)? Is it really the case that people always want to be nudged into healthier lifestyles, as the new paternalists assume (Sugden 2017)? Such questions pose an identification challenge to new paternalists.

Smith's notion of practical reasoning highlights an additional identification challenge. Even if a person feels she has a reasonably stable sense of what she wants, novel situations and contextual elements will incline her to consider previously unanticipated perspectives. Considering such perspectives may incline her to act in a way that appears inconsistent to a spectator, but is really an outcome of a process of rational deliberation and *preference formation* (for discussion of process rationality, see Rizzo and Whitman 2018). Smith's discussion of the contextual nature of the sentiment of approval provides an intuitive justification of the reasonableness of context-dependence and a prima facie defence of apparently inconsistent choices. Smith helps us see that consistency is not a necessary prerequisite for reasonableness, nor should it be expected in many domains of human life (Rescher 1987: 303). Although the reasonableness of inconsistency might not equally challenge all efforts in behavioural welfare economics and new paternalism (Bernheim 2016, 2021; see discussion in Thoma 2021), it makes distinguishing between welfare-relevant and welfare-diminishing choices much more difficult in practice. It raises the epistemic burden of new paternalist practices (Rizzo and Whitman 2009).

## *Dialectics of self-judgement*

Let's consider the dynamics of self-judgement in Smith's account in greater detail. The basic point is that our sentiment of self-approval operates through our lived experience by which we bring an irreducible 'personal coefficient' to bear on specific situations.[10] There is an inarticulable dimension to our judgement of what we want to do. To determine what we really want in a situation requires a situation-specific dialogue between our acting person and the 'man within the breast'. The determination of our preferences in context can only be made by fully entering the

---

10  I take the phrase 'personal coefficient' from Michael Polanyi (1962).

specific situation of choice.[11] Those details require a high degree of contextual knowledge (Haakonssen 1981: 79) and are normally unavailable to onlookers, be they economists or policymakers.

Smith analogises our self-judgement to the way we judge others. The process of self-judgement is 'altogether the same with that by which we exercise ... judgment concerning the conduct of other people' (Smith 1982: 109). The key to judgement is sympathy. Sympathy is not a passive emotional process for Smith; it is a process of imaginary projection, a process of metaphorically becoming the being whom we are assessing in order to gain an adequate sense of that being's lifeworld (Fleischacker 2019: 23–48; Smith 1982: 12). Only when we have developed a contextual understanding, by way of sympathy, of the person whom we wish to judge can we mete out proper judgement. Smith's elaboration of the process of sympathy conveys his 'perspectival conception of humanity' (Fleischacker 2019: 48); it also conveys his conception of our 'dialogical experience of conscience'.[12]

The dialectics of our practical reasoning process emerge as we consider self-judgement as a sympathetic exercise.

---

11  One might also attempt to express Smith's insight about contextual knowledge in terms of intrinsic, extrinsic and reputational incentives, along the lines of Bénabou and Tirole (2006). Each person's action 'reflects an endogenous and unobservable mix of three motivations: *intrinsic, extrinsic*, and *reputational*, which must be inferred from their choices and the context' (ibid.: 1654; italics in original). The difficulty of inferring the interplay of these motivations, and the extent to which a person is acting reasonably in light of her goals, is considerably exacerbated when her goals are not settled but in the process of forming.

12  The phrase 'dialogical experience of conscience' comes from Brown (1992).

At any point in time, even on the supposition that he possesses a stable set of commitments and sentiments, the 'man within' applies his commitments and sentiments in a context-dependent manner. To some extent we can say that the 'man within' continuously reconstitutes the bounds of his commitments as he considers how they apply in new circumstances. The 'man within' does not represent to us a categorical imperative or set of context-independent obligations. He is a feeling being – a judge, not a rule. A judge passes down and applies rules, but only after she has heard arguments from both the plaintiff and defendant. A judge serves to facilitate a critical dialogue over the application and interpretation of a set of rules and principles, derived, at least in the common law tradition, through creative renderings of precedent. So too with the 'man within the breast'. He hears the acting self out, as it were. Through the sympathetic imagination, he enters into the situation of the acting self in order to understand how he ought to behave in the particular situation at hand, given his deepest-to-date rendering of our moral commitments.[13] The 'man within' consults and integrates both the 'facts and the feel' of the case in order to judge (Wincewicz 2018: 71).

The significance of these points for Smith come across in his critique of casuistry. Casuists err in attempting to dictate a set of context-independent, hard-and-fast rules for conduct. To the casuists, Smith (1982: 339) rejoins:

---

13 Brown writes, 'moral discourse is open in that its conclusions can not be predetermined or rule-governed; the making of moral judgement requires a fine attention to the details and peculiarities of the case, and its results cannot be anticipated in any particular instance' (Brown 1992: 236).

> When it is that secrecy and reserve begin to grow into dissimulation? How far an agreeable irony may be carried, and at what precise point it begins to degenerate into a detestable lie? What is the highest pitch of freedom and ease of behaviour which can be regarded as graceful and becoming, and when it is that it first begins to run into a negligent and thoughtless licentiousness? With regard to all such matters, what would hold good in any one case would scarce do so exactly in any other, and what constitutes the propriety and happiness of behaviour varies in every case with the smallest variety of situation. Books of casuistry, therefore, are generally as useless as they are commonly tiresome.

The context of Smith's discussion here is a treatment of the bounds of virtue and moral obligation. He criticises the casuists for attempting to codify virtue into a set of precise rules for every conceivable circumstance. But we can take away a more general point: our personal rules and professed maxims are guidelines, but they often must be reconstituted to accord with unanticipated situations and new revelations.

We might say that new paternalist thinking tends towards casuistry. Like the casuists, the new paternalists seem to take something which is, on most intuitive accounts, vague, indeterminate and contextual and attempt to subject it to inappropriately rigid specifications.[14] The

---

14 This is the main charge that Smith levels at the casuists themselves (Smith 1982: 327).

new paternalists will claim that the axioms of rationality are simply instrumental, pertaining to the relation between preferences and not to preferences themselves. But in imposing a logical structure on rational choice the axioms of rationality make certain specifications about what welfare *is not*, and therefore exclude certain preferences from the category of reasonable, welfare-increasing conduct. That exclusion is casuistic in that it subjects the broad church of reason to a set of formal and exact rules that, whatever their analytical value, fail to capture the richness and dynamism of human deliberation.

## *Revisiting the cafeteria*

The applicability of Smith's dynamic ideas of self-judgement and the challenges they pose to new paternalist policy efforts can be clarified with an example. Consider a cafeteria scene, along the lines of Thaler and Sunstein's (2009: 1–3), and a government official, Rachel. Rachel wants to help individuals make the diet decisions they truly want to make. After consulting with behavioural economists and psychologists, she conducts a survey of cafeteria sales. More desserts are sold than fruits and vegetables. This flies in the face of the fact that consuming high levels of processed sugar is unhealthy, leading to diabetes, obesity and so forth, and that most people want to be healthy and live long lives. The survey data lead Rachel to conclude that many individuals would benefit, by their own estimation, from being nudged into healthier eating habits. She decides to enact a regulation requiring desserts to be placed below eye level, along with a printed display on the negative health effects of sugar consumption.

Rachel's decision to nudge is predicated on the conclusion that diners systematically err in their decision-making and over-indulge their preference for sweets. Even if the conclusion is warranted, is it not immediately clear how Rachel can calibrate her nudge to discourage sugar consumption by just the right amount, balancing the pleasure individuals receive from sugar consumption with their professed preferences for healthy living (Rizzo and Whitman 2009). We could easily imagine a well-intended nudge making people's lives worse by entirely discouraging them from the enjoyment of sweets. But upstream of that important issue is a more fundamental question: is Rachel's conclusion of error warranted? Perhaps. But it will be difficult to tell without tending closely to circumstantial details.

Take an individual, Monica, who in consultation with her conscience commits to abstain from eating processed sugar for the sake of healthier living. Violating that commitment normally brings with it the sting of conscience as her conscience attempts to steel her acting self into her diet. But there might be some situations in which she appears to an external spectator to violate her commitment, yet still earns the full approbation of the conscience. Imagine that Monica takes out a friend or a new client for lunch. Suppose that her lunch partner, who is overweight and clearly self-conscious, selects a piece of pie in the cafeteria line. For reasons we cannot say, Monica orders a piece, too. Did she err? Or suppose that Monica goes out to lunch with her grandmother. While Monica steps out to answer a phone call, her grandmother purchases for her a slice of chocolate cake. Monica enjoys it and enjoys her grandmother's enjoyment in seeing her enjoy it. Again, did she err? Monica indeed violates the letter of her previous commitment. But plausibly she did so while maintaining the approval of her conscience, that is, without regret indicative (at least in Smith's account) of error. Although she would appear to Rachel the regulator to have erred, contextual details would tell otherwise.

One might respond that Monica is clearly responding to normatively relevant contextual effects, and that the new paternalism is concerned only with correcting normatively *irrelevant* contextual effects. But how can we, as onlookers, know which contextual details are relevant and irrelevant? The salience of eye-level chocolate cake might induce Monica's conscience to reconsider her understanding of what healthy and enjoyable living entails. Perhaps she has an epiphany that 'healthy' living entails an increase in present pleasure because life is short and uncertain. (This brings up another point: why should the paternalist automatically assume that expressed preferences for less sugar trump revealed preferences for more? Talk is cheap and can underestimate real opportunity costs (Rizzo and Whitman 2009: 919; Delmotte and Dold 2022: 88–89).) A choice for present pleasure might reveal empathy gaps between her present self and her future self, and perhaps it reveals procrastination (Sugden 2017: 120–21). But it might reveal a genuine reappraisal. Regardless, determining the reason for Monica's apparently inconsistent choice will be difficult. Perhaps she looks as if she is choosing cake merely due to its physical placement, but is really doing so because her lunch partner, who is already seated, purchased cake. There is a heavy empirical burden to overcome to conclude that Monica's decision was an error.

Smith's ideas help us see that we may often be able to discover reasonable explanations for apparently inconsistent behaviour by attention to circumstantial detail. More significantly, they help us understand how inconsistency might in some cases contribute to our well-being. Apparent inconsistency within a certain narrow window of choice (e.g. framing effects, menu-dependence) may be a consequence of different legitimate aspects of our preferences trading off against each other in the moment of choice. We ought to cultivate both what Smith calls the 'soft, the gentle, the amiable virtues, the virtues of candid condescension and indulgent humanity,' but also 'the great, the awful, and respectable, the virtues of self-denial' (Smith 1982: 23). We can adapt Smith's point about virtue to comment on preferences: In what instances our preference for hospitality and agreeableness trump sugar vigilance is a matter of personal knowledge and judgement. We may find it useful to adhere, by and large, to the contours of a general set of rules in such matters, such as 'the common proverbial maxims of prudence'. But 'to affect, however, a very strict and literal adherence to them would evidently be the most absurd and ridiculous pedantry' (Smith 1982: 174).

The challenge at this point applies mainly to those who invoke axioms of consistency (or the idea of consistency generally) to purify preferences. Not all behavioural welfare economists operate on these assumptions, however. Building on work with Antonio Rangel, Douglas Bernheim (2016, 2021) proffers a theoretical approach admitting of the 'prevalence and complexity of context-dependent choice patterns' and conceding that such complexity 'limits our knowledge' of decision-making processes and sometimes hinders us from making 'precise normative statements' (Bernheim 2016: 40, 60). In Bernheim's approach an agent makes a mistake only when her choice is 'predicated on a misunderstanding of the available options and consequences, conditional on [her] available information, and if it conflicts with at least one choice for which no such misunderstanding arises' (Bernheim 2021: 391). In such cases an agent can be said to have made a 'characterization error'. If these criteria are not met, however, the theorist has insufficient grounds to conclude that the agent has erred, even if her decisions appear to be inconsistent.

An upshot of Bernheim's approach is an idea that Johanna Thoma calls the 'non-uniqueness of rational preference', which reflects the idea that our underlying preferences do not conform to axioms of consistency and the understanding that this is not in principle problematic (Thoma 2021: 358). In allowing for inconsistency within what he calls the Welfare-Relevant Domain, Bernheim's approach is an improvement upon other approaches in behavioural welfare economics. Two issues one might still raise with his approach concern our ability in practice to effectively identify characterisation errors and the logical connection between characterisation errors and policy interventions (see Rizzo and Whitman 2020: 275–77). A more general issue, one that Bernheim's approach shares with others, is that his account still appears to conceive of welfare largely in static terms. Smith's framework, however, highlights dynamic aspects of welfare, to which I now turn.

## Our dynamic being within

Some have critiqued the new paternalism (as well as traditional welfare economics) for its reliance on preference satisfaction as a welfare criterion. Across many publications, Robert Sugden has articulated an opportunity criterion of welfare, which builds from the idea that each person would like to have more opportunity than less (see recent discussions in Sugden 2018). Sugden's opportunity criterion presupposes the temporal instability and context dependence of our preferences. He argues there is no good reason to presume that preferences will (or should) conform to neoclassical axioms of rationality. Others emphasise the salience of preference formation over preferences satisfaction in considerations of welfare. Such approaches, as exemplified by Dold (2018), Dold and Schubert (2018) and Dold and Rizzo (2021), build around dynamic conceptions of welfare inspired by such thinkers as James Buchanan, Frank Knight and John Stuart Mill. Dynamic conceptions of welfare suggest that welfare analysis ought to focus on institutions that help individuals develop the capabilities to learn and shape themselves into the people they want to be.

Smith's formulations enhance such discussions. From a Smithian point of view, welfare or well-being is much less about the satisfying of static preferences and much more about upward vitality – the aspiration to become something better, something lovely, something worthy of praise. The desire to better our condition, which features so prominently in Smith's political economy, includes not just the desire for material improvement, but the desire to refine our character, habits and tastes (Fleischacker 2004: 63; Griswold 1999: 130–36; Wincewicz 2018: 64). We desire not simply to do what our 'man within' wants, but to have our 'man within' want right, good and worthwhile things (see Smith 1982: 113).[15] The importance of upward vitality for Smith edifies calls for behavioural welfare economics to look beyond preference satisfaction (e.g. Dold and Rizzo 2021; Dold and Schubert 2018; Schubert 2015) and tend to the institutions and social arrangements that facilitate learning and personal dynamism.

## *Searching after The Impartial Spectator*

One way to capture the dynamic aspects of welfare in Smith is to extend his dialogical metaphor of self-understanding. Social interaction, Smith says, teaches us to think of our person in terms of an acting self and judging self, the 'man within'. We naturally seek the approval our inner judge. But maturation eventually leads us to probe the judgement of our inner judge. Why should we listen

---

15  In this way Smith's thought resembles Frank Knight's idea that what we want is not the satisfaction of our preferences, but having better preferences to satisfy (Knight 1922: 458). The same idea can be discerned in the thought of Smith's friend David Hume (Rotwein 2009: xlvii; Matson 2021c).

to his call to abstain from momentary pleasure? From where does his authority derive? Such questions lead us to place our 'man within' in conversation with another being, an inner-inner judge, so to speak. This judge is The Impartial Spectator.

Throughout TMS Smith employs the phrase 'impartial spectator' in a number of ways (Klein et al. 2018: 1155). At times, 'impartial spectator' designates a literal bystander of an event, a person presumed to be well-wishing, well enough informed, and disinterested in the event's outcome. On occasion, Smith also uses 'man within the breast' and 'the impartial spectator' interchangeably. In the final edition of TMS, however, he repeatedly differentiates between the two (Matson 2021b: 277–78). When he calls the 'man within' an impartial spectator, he frequently modifies the description with the sceptical adjective 'supposed' (think: 'alleged') (e.g. Smith 1982: 131, 134, 145; see Klein et al. 2018: 1162–64). Other times Smith uses the phrase 'impartial spectator' to signify a higher being who possesses knowledge and beneficial judgement above and beyond ordinary capacity (e.g. Smith 1982: 215). On this usage, The Impartial Spectator is a godlike being able to enter the particulars of all our circumstances, with universal benevolence towards the whole of humankind. By capitalising The Impartial Spectator, I emphasise that godlike conception of 'the impartial spectator', which is importantly distinguished from the conception of the 'man within'.[16]

---

16 This polysemous interpretation of 'the impartial spectator' stands at odds with some scholars' interpretations. Raphael contends that 'the impartial spectator is still a man, not a god, and indeed a perfectly normal

The 'man within' plays a representative role in our society of self. He first represents to us the sentiments of our community. He teaches us to govern ourselves through self-dialogue by reference to what he imagines would be the sentiments of representatives of our community, even if no such representatives are literally present at the moment of our choice. But the human spirit is not content with simple conformity to social norms. We long for warranted approbation from worthy spectators (Griswold 1999: 134).[17] We want not just to be praised but to be worthy of the praise we receive; we want to be lovely in addition to being loved (Smith 1982: 113–14). In pursuit of such ideals, the 'man within the breast' attempts to govern the acting self by reference not to the sentiments of the actual spectators in our midst, but to what he imagines '*ought to be* the judgments of others' (Smith 1982: 110; italics added) if they had

man' (Raphael 2007: 13). Campbell says of 'the impartial spectator', 'all his characteristics are fully human, and he possesses these only to the degree which is common in the average person' (Campbell 1971: 137; see also Fleischacker 2016: 274; Smith 2016: 328). These scholars generally identify the 'man within the breast' and 'the impartial spectator' as one and the same, and emphasise the humanness of his identity. Others affirm the presence of a godlike Impartial Spectator, however, along the lines of my interpretation (see, for example, Brown 1994: 74; Evensky 1987: 452; Haakonssen 1981: 56). Some scholars likewise maintain an important distinction between the 'man within the breast' and 'the impartial spectator' (see Young 1997: 74; Den Uyl 2016: 264).

17 'To a real wise man the judicious and well-weighed approbation of a single wise man, gives more heartfelt satisfaction that all the noisy applauses of ten thousand ignorant though enthusiastic admirers. He may say with Parmenides, who, upon reading a philosophical discourse before a public assembly at Athens, and observing, that except Plato, the whole company had left him, continued, notwithstanding, to read on, and said that Plato alone was audience sufficient for him' (Smith 1982: 253).

sufficient wisdom, virtue and knowledge. The 'man within the breast' is by no means steady or infallible in these efforts – the clamor of the crowd and the natural deep desire for social acceptance and praise often sway him from his path.[18] But, nonetheless, he desires to live in accordance with higher standards. In his search after higher standards, the 'man within' represents to us his sense of what The Impartial Spectator approves of.[19]

If The Impartial Spectator, by construction, is a godlike being with superhuman knowledge and beneficence, how is our 'man within', who is 'of mortal extraction' (Smith 1982: 131), to know what he (The Impartial Spectator) approves of? He doesn't, in fact, at least never definitively. The course of his development – the course of *our* development – consists in a continuous exploration about what The Impartial Spectator approves, both inter- and intrapersonally.

Interpersonally we converse, in effect, about moral and aesthetic norms in various modes. Intrapersonally we deliberate about desirable paths of life. I reflect upon what The Impartial Spectator wants *me* to do – how should I live, what should my tastes be, how I should govern my conduct? The question has obvious theological overtones, and,

---

18 See, for example, Smith's short analysis of self-deception (Smith 1982: 156–59), and his discussion conflicts between 'the man without' and 'the man within' (130–32).

19 See especially Smith (1982: 215), where he described the 'man within the breast' as the 'representative of the impartial spectator'. Elsewhere, he writes of our 'man within the breast' as 'the supposed impartial spectator of our conduct', who appeals to 'a still higher tribunal, to that of the all-seeing Judge of the world' (131). See also his comment about our inchoate idea of perfection and the role of the man within helping us both solidify that idea and progress towards it (247).

indeed, for religious individuals it is analogous with the question 'what does God want me to do?' But it is generalisable to all different beliefs, including non-religious. On a non-theological interpretation, The Impartial Spectator is simply a metaphorical being who takes on all the character traits that we have learned, through experience with actual humans, to associate with our highest conception of goodness, wisdom and right judgement. The Impartial Spectator on the non-theological account will naturally resemble the best parts of our exemplars, teachers and heroes. The Impartial Spectator, in other words, embodies our conception of wisdom and virtue. Through his judgements he brings wisdom and virtue on specific choice situations.

A critic might wonder at this point what The Impartial Spectator has to do with sugar consumption, smoking, retirement contributions and gym routines – the workaday concerns of behavioural economists. One answer is that The Impartial Spectator metaphor is a useful way to think about the complexity of our preferences, even the mundane ones. Drawing out the idea that we want to do what our 'man within' wants to do, and that our 'man within' wants to do what The Impartial Spectator wants to do, highlights how our preferences, over a meaningful domain of circumstances, are not very well-defined and are often in process. This observation reinforces the discussion about the potential reasonableness of inconsistency. In addition to signalling the trading off of active perspectives at the moment of choice, inconsistency over time might evidence a process of learning and discovery, a process of becoming. Perhaps the actor is, as Mill would have it, conducting 'experiments in living' (Mill 2003: 122) or 'preference rotations' in an effort to discover what conduces to her own good (Rizzo and Whitman 2020: 59–60).

Another answer is that decisions about sugar consumption, smoking, retirement planning and exercise, mundane though they are, are all part of living a life. Our sublime ideals are not so separable from mundane decisions about our personal well-being as we might sometimes think (see discussion in Sunstein 2020: 204–5; see also Knight 1922). Day to day, our ideals come into contact with the mundane as we deliberate over small things in service of higher preferences. Decisions about diet and savings might appear trivial or unidimensional on their face; but they entail various trade-offs across many margins, tradeoffs concerning things like enjoyment, hospitality, agreeableness, sociability, present and future financial comfort, charitable giving, physical and mental health, self-image, and family. Considerations about such matters involve larger questions about who we think we should be and why. They may, in other words, reasonably be framed as questions about the approval of The Impartial Spectator.

## Error and affirmation

Smith's ideas help us distinguish between two sorts of error: (1) when we act in a way that brings on the disapproval of the 'man within' and (2) when the judgement of the 'man within' fails to correspond to the judgement of The Impartial Spectator. Both sorts of error are relevant to considerations about welfare, but they are important to distinguish conceptually. The first type of error is *relatively* static. It occurs when we fail to satisfy preferences that we currently hold. The second sort of error occurs when we fail to satisfy preferences that we do not yet hold but are in the process of discovering. Both sorts of error are difficult to identify from an external perspective, which raises challenges for new paternalist–style policies. Inconsistency, as discussed above, is no sure identifier of the first sort of error, because different choice frames might elicit new perspectives on the objects of choice. Discerning the second sort of error involves discursive considerations of the good, which of course is no exact science.[20]

Another issue is that these types of errors might interact in real time. Even as we reflect on how our preferences cash out in specific situations, through dialogue with our 'man within', the perspectives of our 'man within' are changing as he seeks out The Impartial Spectator. The interaction effect here points to significant challenges to identifying erroneous preferences. One must gather a good deal of contextual information before formulating a judgement about whether a person's behaviour errs from the person's own perspective.

On reflection, it might seem that the interaction of our acting self, the 'man within', and The Impartial Spectator presents challenges for our own sense of development and self-improvement. Smith maintains that we err when we feel the disapproval of our 'man within'. But the 'man

---

20 I'm indebted to an anonymous referee for bringing the insights in this paragraph to my attention.

within' is constantly in process as he imagines and deliberates over the character of The Impartial Spectator. How can our learning – and often fallible! – 'man within' serve as a standard for choice? How can we, at any given moment, cogently speak of 'error' or 'improvement' if we lack a fixed point from which such concepts derive meaning?

There are no easy answers to such questions. We must, I think, have recourse to a pragmatic notion of self-affirmation. At every moment we face some uncertainty regarding the course of our future development. Yet we constantly affirm our deepest-to-date values and convictions, drawing upon them as a relatively fixed point from which we self-assess, all the while recalling, at a subsidiary level, that our values and convictions are more fluid than we pretend. To draw on ideas advanced by Frank Knight and James Buchanan, perhaps we perceive our preferences as 'relatively absolute absolutes', a formulation which, much like Smith's ideas of the impartial spectator,[21] 'avoids the coziness of both the relativist and the absolutists at the cost of taking on attributes of Janus, attributes of a necessary duality in outlook' (Buchanan 1999: 443). Our values and corresponding commitments will never 'be really absolute, for they [are] never cut loose entirely from the real world and its possibilities of growth and transformation'

---

21 Over the different editions of *The Theory of Moral Sentiments*, Smith struggles and attempts to dissolve the tension between the relative and the absolute. If our idea of The Impartial Spectator is socially informed, how can our idea of the good rise above social custom? Is virtue merely a crowd-dependent phenomena? For discussion of these tensions, see Forman-Barzilai (2010: 96–104).

(Knight 1923: 583). Yet, bearing responsibility for our errors in our affirmations, we affirm our commitments and speak meaningfully enough to ourselves through the sentiment of regret about genuine errors in our actions.

To again revisit the cafeteria: when Monica has an epiphany that life is short and to be enjoyed, and accordingly decides to eat a piece of cake against her previous commitments, she affirms her current preference as a part of herself and as appropriate given the path she has selected. She might later reevaluate and determine that her decision was an error. But that responsibility and affirmation are hers alone, part of her learning process and sense of self.

## Implications and conclusions

My principal aim in this chapter has been to use Smith's ideas to draw out some epistemic and practical difficulties facing new paternalist–style policymaking. These difficulties lie partly in the fact that inconsistency is not inherently unreasonable. Inconsistency might signal the interplay in a given moment between disjointed perspectives on an object of choice. It could also be a sign that a person is deliberating over the character of The Impartial Spectator. Inconsistency cannot, in general, be used as a criterion for differentiating between welfare-increasing and decreasing choice.

In addition, the idea from Smith that we desire discursive self-improvement poses a constructive methodological suggestion for welfare economics generally. It edifies calls for economists interested in welfare issues to look away from preference satisfaction as such and toward the institutional arrangements and social factors that best enable one to develop into the person he or she wants to be. An important suggestion along these lines is Robert Sugden's opportunity criterion. A central justification of the criterion is that there is value in leaving as much room as possible for agents to satisfy future preferences, given that each agent is not entirely certain of what he will prefer in the future and who he will become. Another suggestion by Malte Dold and Christian Schubert calls for us to consider how people develop preferences and conceive of their own agency and to formulate policy design accordingly. Conceiving of individuals as 'loci of learning', Dold and Schubert call for institutional reform so as to not 'hinder individuals from reconstituting themselves' (Dold and Schubert 2018: 234).

Smith's ideas are again instructive in this context. His treatise on political economy and public policy (*The Wealth of Nations*) flows out of his investigations of moral psychology, sociology and ethics in TMS (see Smith 1982: 342). We can consider the 'the liberal plan of equality, liberty, and justice' (Smith 1981: 664) as Smith's central statement of the appropriate inclinations in public policy given his ideas of the dynamism of human nature in TMS (McRorie 2023). Freedom within an 'equal and impartial administration of justice' (Smith 1981: 610) is what he believed would best allow each to better his or her condition, in material and non-material terms.

A lengthy discussion of the connections between Smith's liberal plan, ideas about welfare and vision of human nature is not possible here.²² But I will briefly make several basic points. First, Smith believed that freedom facilitates commerce, commerce facilitates social interaction, and social interaction facilitates multi-perspective deliberation and the development of self-command (see Paganelli 2010). Exchange leads to relationships among strangers. Even if they are only transactional, those relationships require us to exercise a degree of sympathy and restraint. Exercises in sympathy teach us to command our passions and bring them to a level that others can go along with. In a free society, as we interact with jural equals under the law, we are time and again drawn back to 'the great school of self-command' by which we study to be 'more master' of ourselves (Smith 1982: 145). The lessons we learn from interactions with others are formative in our development of preferences and conception of The Impartial Spectator. They also gradually provide us with the wherewithal and command to pursue and cultivate those developing preferences. Smith smiles upon larger opportunity sets, so to speak, because they give rise to more opportunity for social interaction, reflection and self-development.

Second, along the lines of Dold and Schubert (2018) Smith shows himself eager to reform policies that prohibit individuals from reconstitution and self-improvement. He makes a strong case for things like free choice in occupation, free trade in land, free internal trade and free commerce (Viner 1927: 213). These are advanced, of course,

---

22 For useful discussions, see Muller (1993), Young (1997), Otteson (2002), Fleischacker (2004) and Hanley (2009).

primarily on economic grounds. But when we understand that Smith's main concern in economic reform is allowing each to better his condition or pursue 'his own interest his own way' (Smith 1981: 664), and that bettering one's condition involves moral and aesthetic improvement, the connection between economic policy and upward vitality can be sustained. Freedom is a main institutional prerequisite to self-improvement for Smith. Freedom is not the only prerequisite, for Smith understands that sometimes individual's learning capabilities and civic awareness may be underdeveloped due extreme extensions of the division of labour (Smith 1981: 782). In such instances, his approach is to consider ways that policy can help facilitate the development of individuals' faculties, for example, through the localised provision of primary education.

Kenneth Boulding once said that Adam Smith 'has a strong claim to being both the Adam and the Smith' of economics (Boulding 1969: 1). To conclude this essay, let me say that I agree, and that I believe that tending to Smith's ideas, perhaps especially the interplay between his two great works, might be a fruitful way to advance in conversations about human behaviour and public policy. I've argued here that Smithian ideas about self-awareness, self-judgement and welfare challenge aspects of behavioural welfare economics and new paternalism. But it also seems to me that reading *The Wealth of Nations* with ideas about the dynamic and psychological aspects of human nature in mind could yield interesting insights that dovetail with philosophical and methodological research in behavioural economics.

## 3 SATISFACTION IN ACTION: HUME'S ENDOGENOUS THEORY OF PREFERENCES AND THE VIRTUES OF COMMERCE

David Hume's analysis of the passions and his account of sympathy prefigure a number of developments in contemporary psychology (see Reed 2018). His *Political Discourses*, which one of his earlier biographers referred to as 'the cradle of political economy' (Burton 1846, 1:354), showcase a sophisticated understanding of consumption, trade and monetary dynamics, along with an appreciation for the social and historical embeddedness of economic activity (Skinner 2009; see also Schabas and Wennerlind 2008). The connections between these areas of Hume's thought are understudied relative to their importance and contemporary relevance.[1] The connections can perhaps inform

---

1 For some recent work in this vein, see Wennerlind (2011) and Grüne-Yanoff and McClennen (2008). For earlier treatments, see, for example, Rotwein (2009) and Hirschman (2013). In his comprehensive introduction to Hume's economic essays, Eugene Rotwein (2009) divides Hume's economics into three subsections: economic psychology, political economy and economic philosophy. Rotwein's section on economic psychology is detailed, drawing extensively on Hume's analysis of the passions in his *Treatise of Human Nature*. But the connections between Hume's psychology and his economic philosophy are not emphasised. Psychology also plays an important role in Albert Hirschman's (2013) treatment of Hume in *The Passions and the Interests*. But he doesn't delve into the social dimension of Hume's psychology at great length.

ongoing efforts to integrate insights from psychology and philosophy into political economy, especially with respect to questions of preference formation, welfare and economic policy.

This chapter traces connections between what might be called Hume's theory of preferences and his economic philosophy. Drawing from Hume's account of the passions in Book 2 of his *Treatise of Human Nature* (especially his account of pride and sympathy), I argue that, from the standpoint of contemporary economic theory, Hume has what could be considered an endogenous theory of preferences. He views preferences as comparative desires that are formed through and continually affected by interpersonal processes of sympathy. Sympathy in Hume explains how preferences are formed through socialisation and cultural processes. Although they adapt based upon individuals' interpretations of feasibility (Elster 2016: 110–41), preferences are affected and even elicited by – and hence, endogenous to – social framing. Hume has within his account the resources to explain why, for instance, leadership, persuasion, social identity and considerations of status affect choice. Choice always occurs within a social frame of reference that affects decision (cf. Fehr and Hoff 2011).

After sketching Hume's theory of preferences, I point to conceptual connections between that theory and the framework of his political economy. Hume's theory of preferences in some way resembles the thinking of both modern behavioural and experimental economists (cf. Bowles 1998) and older institutionalist economists like Thorstein Veblen. But whereas some behavioural economists and institutionalists emphasise welfare-decreasing aspects of free commercial society, Hume maintains a largely optimistic attitude. Commercial society, he says, features an 'indissoluble chain' of *industry, knowledge,* and *humanity* (EMPL 271; italics in original).[2] The ages of commerce are both the happiest and the most virtuous (EMPL 269). I argue here that Hume's views about commercial society, and his economic philosophy generally, are not independent but build from his psychology, from his theory of the passions. A key to the connection is that like Frank Knight (1922), Hume understands happiness or well-being – concepts which are largely coextensive in his thought – to lie largely in the process of satisfying one's preferences rather than in the state of having one's preferences satisfied. On such an understanding, the comparative and sympathetic nature of preferences need not be taken as sources of dissatisfaction as, for example, they are in Veblen. Context-dependent preferences can be interpreted, under the right institutional arrangements, as providing a fund for purposeful actions – ideas, aspirations and new ends towards which the individual can actively strive. Hume sees commercial society as providing an open set of new

---

2 Abbreviations to Hume's texts are as follows. References to *A Treatise of Human Nature* are to Hume (2007), abbreviated as 'T', followed by book, part, section and paragraph. References to *An Enquiry Concerning Human Understanding* or the *First Enquiry* are to Hume (2000), abbreviated as 'EHU', followed by section, part (when one exists) and paragraph. References to *An Enquiry Concerning the Principles of Morals* or the *Second Enquiry* are to Hume (1998), abbreviated as 'EPM', followed by section, part (when one exists) and paragraph. References to the *Essays: Moral, Political, and Literary* are to Hume (1994), abbreviated as 'EMPL', followed by page.

ends, driven by sympathy and social comparison, that channel individuals' energy and desire. Hume's essays on commerce, especially 'Of Commerce' and 'Of Refinement in the Arts', support such an interpretation. In addition to drawing out an interesting conception of happiness, these connections enhance our understanding of Hume's dynamic perspective of commerce as not merely a process of satisfying an 'existing array of wants', but of 'creating new and refined tastes' (Boyd 2008: 83).

## Hume on preferences

Hume doesn't have a theory of 'preferences' as such, simply because he doesn't use the term 'preference' or 'preferences' systematically in his work. When he does occasionally use such terms, he sometimes does so to indicate a comparison of ideas on the basis of feeling: 'When I give the *preference* to one set of arguments over another, I do nothing but decide from my feeling concerning the superiority of their influence' (T 1.3.8.12; italics added).[3] Other times he uses 'preferences' to indicate favoured practices (e.g. EPM 5.2.42). But insofar as a theory of preferences can be understood as a theory of human action derived from an account of desires and beliefs, it is clear that Hume has one.

What we might call Hume's theory of preferences lies in his account of the passions, which he takes to be the 'ultimate motivations' and 'fundamental *explanans*' of

---

3 This particular assertion refers to Hume's idea that belief is largely non-cognitive. Whether or not we believe X is a matter of the manner in which we conceive X, not a matter of the content of X itself (T 1.3.8).

human action (Grüne-Yanoff and McClennen 2008: 88; italics in original). It is easiest to understand the passions in the context of Hume's theory of mind. At the outset of his *Treatise* he distinguishes between two types of mental perceptions: impressions and ideas. The difference between impressions and ideas is a matter of strength or 'liveliness' (T 1.1.1.1). It is perhaps useful, if not entirely accurate, to say that whereas impressions are *felt*, ideas are *thought*. The basis for this distinction is that ideas are imagined representations or copies of prior impressions that are stripped of their lively qualities (T 1.1.1.7). To illustrate the point, Hume remarks that 'when I shut my eyes and think of my chamber, the ideas I form are exact representations of the impressions I felt' (T 1.1.1.3).

The passions are a certain class of impressions called 'reflective impressions' that are distinguished from sensory or 'original' impressions (T 2.1.1.1). Whereas sensory impressions are feelings caused by 'the constitution of the body, [...] animal spirits, or [...] the application of objects to external organs' (T 2.1.1.1), reflective impressions or passions are feelings triggered in response to ideas of past experience. The passions are often ontogenetically related to sensory impressions. Consider a simple example. If a child touches a fire, she will instinctively feel a sensory impression of pain. Subsequently, reflecting upon the idea of touching fire will likely induce a painful mental state of fear – a passion – in connection with the memory of previous pain.

Hume's theory of psychological association is at the centre of his treatment of the passions. The essence of his theory of association is that previous impressions, through the faculty of memory, bring to mind impressions that they resemble; ideas, through the faculty of imagination, bring to mind other ideas related by relations of resemblance, contiguity, and cause and effect. The memory of enjoying an ice cream cone, for example, presently brings to mind a pleasant impression. The idea of an ice cream cone will also likely call to mind ideas related by resemblance, spatial and temporal contiguity, and cause and effect: ideas of ice cream parlours, summertime, air conditioning, sunshine, satisfying one's sweet tooth, and so forth.

A central feature of any theory of preferences is that preferences, however understood in their particulars, play a central role in motivating an individual's choices. In economics, preferences are, given constraints and technology, typically assumed to uniquely determine choice. That assumption has changed some with the advent of behavioural economics over the past few decades, in which choices are not simply determined by preferences, but affected by various psychological shocks which distract one from acting in line with one's true preferences. But the standard economic interpretation of preferences holds that individuals choose, or act in line with, what they most prefer. As Daniel Hausman (2012: 15) puts it, 'among the alternatives they believe to be available, agents will choose one that is at the top of their preference ranking'. Going back to Paul Samuelson, and following the revealed-preference theory tradition, many economists even go so far as to take choice, irrespective of belief, to be coextensive with preference. Preferences on such an understanding can be simply inferred from observation of individual choice, and, in the aggregate, from price movements and data.[4]

In drawing out Hume's theory of preferences from his account of the passions, then, we need to focus on the specific type of passions that he sees as directly actuating the will. That type is the group of passions he calls 'the direct passions' (T 2.1.1.4). The direct passions stand in distinction to the indirect passions. Whereas the indirect passions rely on a double relation of ideas and impressions (discussed further below), the direct passions arise 'from good [i.e. pleasure] and evil [i.e. pain] most naturally, and with the least preparation'; they include the passions of 'desire and aversion, grief and joy, hope and fear, along with volition' (T 2.3.9.1). For present purposes the most important of the direct passions is desire. Hume uses 'desire', 'will', and 'volition' somewhat interchangeably. He speaks, for example, of a 'new force to our desire or volition' (T 2.3.9.4). Desire arises from 'good consider'd simply' (T 2.3.9.7). On perceiving an idea that we subconsciously associate in the memory with a previous pleasant impression, we may feel a present desire or motivation to realise that pleasure once again. In other words, desire directly leads to action by inducing an individual to pursue the objects of desire. The idea of eating an ice cream cone on a hot summer's day, associated in the memory with the pleasing impression derived from eating an ice cream cone last week, will likely give rise to the desire to eat ice cream today, which will encourage one to eat ice cream.

---

4 The simple identification of preferences with choice, without the intermediation of belief, is problematic. For an elaboration of this argument, see Hausman (2012: 23–33).

How does Hume's understanding of desire align with the standard interpretation of preferences in economics? There are three issues that are to be considered: rationality, phenomenology and content. The first two are helpful in understanding the distinctive character, from the perspective of modern economics, of Hume's account. The third issue is the most significant for connections between Hume's theory of preferences and his assessment of commerce.

Hausman (2012: 2) interprets preferences in modern economics as 'total comparative evaluation[s]', that is, choice-affecting comparisons of alternative actions, their consequences and states of affairs that '[take] into account *every* consideration the agent judges to be relevant' (italics in original). Preferences on such an understanding are propositional in that they treat 'mental states as representing, expressing, or implying [linguistic] propositions', propositions that are by nature subject to logical analysis (Sugden 2006: 370). As Frank Knight (1922: 456) once put the point, 'economics has always treated desires or motives [i.e. preferences] as facts, of a character susceptible to statement in propositions.' Within such a view of preferences, therefore, lies a 'fragmentary theory of rationality' (Hausman 2012: 13). Such a theory of rationality consists not in the particular content, but in the logical implications of various propositions about preferences, for instance, concerning their transitivity.[5]

---

5 In addition to the logical requirement of transitivity, preferences on the usual interpretation (i.e. the interpretation of neoclassical economics and rational choice theory) are also assumed to be complete and

Hume's account bears little resemblance in this first respect to contemporary theory. There is no theory of rationality latent in his account of desires themselves. This is because desires (and the passions in general) for Hume are, as Robert Sugden (2006) has argued, non-propositional. They are mental states that do not represent, express or imply propositions. Put another way, the passions for Hume have no logical referents; they are simply feelings that arise from various psychological associations. Hume at one point refers to them as 'original existence[s]' that contain 'not any representative quality, which render [them copies] of any other existence or modification' (T 2.3.3.4). Understanding Hume's view of desires as non-propositional implies that inconsistent or intransitive preferences are not necessarily irrational. Hume in fact makes this point almost directly. In a famous passage, he writes (T 2.3.3.6; italics in original):

> 'Tis not contrary to reason to prefer the destruction of the whole world to the scratching of my finger. 'Tis not contrary to reason for me to choose my total ruin, to prevent the least uneasiness of an *Indian* or person wholly unknown to me. 'Tis as little contrary to reason for me to prefer even my own acknowledg'd lesser good to my

---

context-independent. These assumptions and the corresponding understanding of rationality were originally made for modelling purposes, i.e. to enable the construction of a continuous, order-preserving utility function. They are now often used, however, especially in behavioural economics, as a standard for how consumers ought to, and indeed truly desire to, behave (Rizzo 2017).

> greater, and have more ardent affection for the former than the latter.[6]

The last sentence shows Hume indicating that pursuing short-term gain at the expense of one's recognised long-term interest is not contrary to reason. This is an especially notable assertion in light of recent developments in behavioural economics and assertions that individuals are irrationally myopic, weak-willed and short-sighted. Such conclusions are not warranted by Hume's theory. By Hume's theory of psychological association, it would actually be surprising if people did not exhibit behaviour that violated strictures of transitivity and were not, for instance, subject to framing effects.[7]

But it is important to note that Hume in the above passage is *not* saying that one can rationally pursue whatever ends one prefers (like the destruction of the world or the scratching of a finger). He does not, as Sugden (2006: 376) emphasises, here evince a theory of instrumental rationality. His point in the passage is rather that the judgements of reason – in the particular sense of the word that refers to our inferential faculty and its activities of demonstrative and probable reasoning – simply *do not apply* to the

---

[6] Note that Hume's uses of 'prefer' here could easily be substituted with 'desire'.

[7] Hume himself speaks to the natural variability, even inconsistency, of desire at a number of points across his works. In his *Essays*, he says: 'To some it appears matter of still more surprise, that a man should differ so widely from himself at different times; and, after possession, reject with disdain what, before, was the object of all his vows and wishes' (EMPL 155; see also EMPL 256).

passions.[8] Reason, taken as an inferential mental faculty, 'is, and ought only to be the slave of the passions, and can never pretend [claim] to any other office than to serve and obey them' (T 2.3.3.4). He seems to slightly qualify his assertion by noting that a passion might be considered unreasonable if it is based on a false belief, i.e. a belief that misapprehends some matter of fact, or if we select inappropriate means for pursuing the object of passion. But to call the passions themselves unreasonable is short for saying that the judgements which accompany the passions are unreasonable: 'In short, a passion must be accompany'd with some false judgment, in order to its being unreasonable; and even then 'tis not the passion, properly speaking, which is unreasonable, but the judgment' (T 2.3.3.6).[9]

After these issues of rationality, it is useful to consider phenomenology. The term 'phenomenology' here refers to how the mind is understood to experience various mental phenomena. By the standard interpretation, preferences in economics are taken to be experienced by the

---

8  'Reason' in another sense, taken as 'that which one feels others feel to be reasonable', does apply to the passions – but it is itself in fact a kind of passion. On the general polysemy of Hume's use of 'reason' and its implications for his thought, see Matson (2017).

9  This does not, contrary to how it initially comes across, imply that individuals don't have reasons for their actions or passions, or that Hume has no sense of practical reason in his thought. But it does suggest that reasons for passions will always have reference to an irreducible feeling of one sort or another, although those feelings can be deliberately refined through reflection and reason-like activities of the imagination. Such activities result in what Hume calls 'calm passions', which so resemble reason that the two are often conflated (T 2.3.3.8). On feeling-based reasons and the passionate nature of Hume's conception of practical reason, see Schafer (2008).

individual in a kind of mental equilibrium.¹⁰ This is not to say that the content of preferences themselves is calm or tranquil, but rather that the relationship between preferences is stable, well-defined and independent of the way in which decisions are framed. Individuals know what they want and proceed in a decisive, calculative fashion to pursue those wants on the basis of expected utility. Hume's interpretation of desire is again quite different. He conceives the mind to be in something like a perpetual state of flux between various desires; mental activity is largely composed of waves of different interacting passions, with intermittent reflection. He writes in Book I of the *Treatise* (T 1.4.6.4):

> The mind is a kind of theatre, where several perceptions successively make their appearance; pass, re-pass, glide away, and mingle in an infinite variety of postures and situations. [...] They are successive perceptions only, that constitute the mind; nor have we the most distant notion of the place, where the scenes are represented, or of the materials, of which it is compos'd.

---

10 Again, behavioural economists hold a different interpretation. On the behavioural understanding, true preferences – what an individual actually wants – are posited to be calmly held in mental equilibrium. They are the preferences that an individual experiences (or would experience) when she possesses 'full attention, complete information, unlimited cognitive abilities, and self-control' (Thaler and Sunstein 2009: 5). But individuals are often swayed from their true preferences by psychological shocks. Their outer psychological shell prevents them from realising their true preferences, preferences that seem to be held by something resembling an inner rational neoclassical agent (Infante et al. 2016)

As he illustrates here, perceptions come and go on the basis of association. The passions are an important class of such perceptions, and desires are a type of passion. Desires, as all perceptions, come and go on the basis of situation, history and trains of complex associations. Moment to moment, therefore, we might expect desires to change: instability, intransitivity and framing effects are a natural implication, in some cases, of Hume's psychology.

Also important is that Hume conceives of desires *within each moment* to be experienced in a somewhat turbulent fashion. We often experience multiple desires simultaneously, desires with different implications for choice. The course of the passions within the mind at a given point in time is not a unity, but a dynamic plurality. At one point, in his interesting section on the idea of personal identity, Hume helpfully compares the soul to a republic (T 1.4.6.19):

> In this respect, I cannot compare the soul more properly to any thing than to a republic or commonwealth, in which the several members are united by the reciprocal ties of government and subordination, and give rise to other persons, who propagate the same republic and the incessant changes of its parts. And as the same individual republic may not only change its members, but also its laws and constitutions; in like manner the same person may vary his character and disposition, as well as his impressions and ideas, without losing his identity.

As with policy decisions in a republic, what an individual actually does at any given moment is determined by the strongest mental faction, as it were, the strongest of conflicting desires. John Immerwahr (1994: 230) refers to Hume's view in these matters as the 'theory of the predominant passion'.[11]

## Pride and the sympathetic formation of preferences

Economists normally assume that the content of preferences is subjective. Preferences are assumed to express values and attitudes that bear no necessary connection to features of the external world. People like what they like and want what they want. For Hume, however, the content of one's desires (or preferences; the two terms are hereafter used interchangeably) is, at a level relevant to social analysis, causally connected to one's physical but particularly social environment. Hume expresses his understanding of this point, noting, 'the skin, pores, muscles, and nerves of a day-labourer are different from those of a man of quality: So too are his sentiments, actions, and manners. *The different stations of life influence the whole fabric, internal and external*' (T 2.3.1.9; italics added). Modern theorists might therefore say that Hume holds an endogenous theory of preferences. The content of an individual's desires, desires she brings to bear in social processes, are not independent but a product of those processes themselves. It is, again, reasonable to consider preferences for Hume to be endogenous rather than, say, adaptive, because they are affected not only

---

11 For a nice discussion on intrapersonal dynamics of the passions in Hume, see Grüne-Yanoff and McClennen (2008: 91–93).

by long-run socialisation and estimations of feasibility, but by the immediate context of choice, through sympathy.

Hume's description of desire as arising from 'good consider'd simply' is misleading in that it portrays our pleasurable associations as a simple, self-evident matter (T 2.3.9.7). But this is not the case. Our desires are intimately related to what Hume calls the indirect passions, which involve social context and sympathy. Jane McIntyre (2000) argues that we should understand the direct passions as causally related to the indirect passions. She notes that, for Hume, our desires 'are always embedded in, and emerge from, the associative and sympathetic context of the indirect passions' (McIntyre 2000: 82).

What are the indirect passions? Hume first describes them in relation to the direct passions.[12] 'By direct passions,' he says, 'I understand such as arise immediately from good or evil, from pain or pleasure. By indirect such as proceed from the same principles, but by the conjunction of objects' (T 2.1.1.3). He later describes them as passions produced by a certain framework of association, a framework that he calls a 'double relation of ideas and impressions' (T 2.1.5.5). The ideas involved in this relation are objects (things toward which an indirect passion is directed) and causes (things which, by virtue of association with the object, sparks an indirect passion). The impressions involved are the feelings evoked by the perceived quality of the cause and the feeling evoked by the association between cause and object. The second impression is the indirect passion

---

12 On Hume's account of the indirect passions, see Taylor (2015: 1–31).

itself. There are two potential objects of the indirect passions: the self and others. There are two potential qualities of the causes of the indirect passions: pleasant or painful. There are, therefore, four principal indirect passions: pride, humility, love and hate (shown in Figure 1). A person will feel the passion of pride if he or she associates something that is independently pleasing with himself or herself. A person will feel the passion of humility if he or she associates something that is independently displeasing with himself or herself. A person will feel the passion of love if he or she associates something that is independently pleasing with some other person. A person will feel the passion of hate if he or she associates something that is independently displeasing with some other person.[13]

A notable feature of Hume's account of the indirect passions is that he formulates them entirely in terms of efficient causes. Unlike some of his predecessors, for example, Francis Hutcheson and Joseph Butler, Hume's account of the passions is non-teleological (Taylor 2015: 30). Moreover, he does not think that similar experiences and objects necessarily lead to similar motivations throughout history – something of which he is sometimes accused of on the

---

13  To say that I feel the passion of hate or love because I associate someone with something displeasing or pleasing, like an ugly or beautiful shirt, sounds jarring to modern ears. But Hume is intentionally using these words in ways that differ from their colloquial uses. In the tradition of Christian virtue, for instance, pride is considered a vice, whereas humility is a virtue. Hume turns these tables entirely, maintaining that pride can be virtuous and, indeed, can be an important motivation to virtue (see Besser-Jones 2010). He derides humility, on the other hand, placing it alongside the train of useless 'monkish' virtues (EPM 9.1.3).

basis of a quick reading of a few passages in his text. He can accommodate wide degrees of historical and cultural variation within his theory (see Forbes 1975: 102–21; Taylor 2015: 35–38). Hume's agnosticism about the causes of the indirect passions and his sense of their cultural variability comes across clearly in his early discussion of pride and humility. He remarks (T 2.1.3.5; italics in original):

> But tho' the causes of pride and humility be plainly *natural*, we shall find upon examination, that they are not *original*, and that 'tis utterly impossible they shou'd each of them be adapted to these passions by a particular provision, and primary constitution of nature. Besides their prodigious number, many of them are the effects of art, and arise partly from the industry, partly from the caprice, and partly from the good fortune of men. Industry produces houses, furniture, cloaths. Caprice determines their particular kinds and qualities. And good fortune frequently contributes to all this, by discovering the effects that result from the different mixtures and combinations of bodies.[14]

But despite this great variation in potential causes, actual causes of the indirect passions in time and place have

---

14 Note here how Hume understands the causes of the indirect passions to be determined by social processes including art and industry. In some important respects, his thought on these matters resembles the ideas of twentieth-century American institutionalists, including Veblen, J. M. Clark and Galbraith. I discuss some aspects of such resemblance below. For some general remarks on Hume's historical method in connection with the institutionalists, see Skinner (2009).

natural limitations by virtue of Hume's theory of mind, which he does take to be universal. It is because of such natural limitations that he says in the above passage that the causes of pride 'be plainly *natural*' (T 2.1.3.5; italics in original). These limitations point to the way that an individual's passions are educated and shed light on the way social norms and standards are formed.

Figure 1   The four principal indirect passions

|  | Quality of cause is pleasant | Quality of cause is painful |
|---|---|---|
| Object of cause is the self | 1. Pride | 2. Humility |
| Object of cause is someone else | 3. Love | 4. Hate |

Hume at one point speaks of four limitations of the causes of pride. The first limitation is that an object, to cause the passion of pride, must be closely related to ourselves (T 2.1.6.3). He gives the example of a feast. We feel the direct passion of joy on attending a feast; but it is usually only the master or the host who feels pride in the feast.[15] A shirt that I take to be beautiful may be an object of conditional pride, in the sense that I imagine that

---

15 Hume admits, "'Tis true, men sometimes boast of a great entertainment, at which they have only been present; and by so small a relation convert their pleasure into pride' (T 2.1.6.2). But he thinks that this is unusual.

I would feel proud if I possessed it. But it is not a proper cause of pride unless I sufficiently associate it with myself, for example, until I wear it. The second limitation is that in order to cause pride an object must be peculiarly related to ourselves. This second limitation relates to Hume's view that the way we feel about ourselves is naturally a matter of comparison to our feelings about others.[16] We typically take no pride in our health, unless it is far above average. Average health 'is seldom regarded as a subject of vanity, because 'tis shared with such vast numbers' (T 2.1.6.5). A third limitation is that the cause of pride must generally be durable: 'what is casual and inconstant gives but little joy, and less pride' (T 2.1.6.6). A final limitation (third on Hume's list at T 2.1.6.5) is perhaps the most important. It is that 'the pleasant and painful object [the cause of pride or humility] be very discernible and obvious, and that not only to ourselves, but to others also. [...] We fancy ourselves more happy, as well as more virtuous or beautiful, when we appear so to others' (T 2.1.6.6).

The point that an object will only cause pride if we perceive (i.e. if we believe) that it pleases others points to a social epistemology in Hume's view of the passions. Hume sees that our emotional bearing in the world is, by and large, a matter of repeated social interaction and the interpersonal communication of ideas.[17] Our indirect

---

16 On the importance of interpersonal comparison in the operation of the passions, see especially T 2.2.8 and T 3.3.2.

17 Hume's account of the understanding in Book 1 of the *Treatise* also evinces something like a social epistemology. As Nicholas Capaldi (1989: 22) expresses this, 'Instead of attempting to scrutinize our thought process in

passions, and by extension our preferences, are fundamentally affected by our beliefs and perceptions about what objects bring other people pleasure and pain. Thus, while the possible efficient causes of pride may be innumerable (any particular sense of what constitutes virtue, beauty, pleasure and goodness might underlie one's experience of pride and desire), an individual's sense of pride is deeply shaped by culture and her understanding of the attitudes of those around her (Taylor 2015: 34). To put the point another way, although our desires or preferences arise from 'good consider'd simply' (T 2.3.9.7), our sense of what constitutes the good, what qualities in objects and character are pleasing, is derived from our social experience and our sense of what we imagine pleases and pains others. Hume goes so far as to say that any cause of the indirect passions have 'little influence, when not seconded by the opinions and sentiments of others' (T 2.1.11.1).

In terms of Hume's psychology, the key to his social epistemology is sympathy: 'sympathy provides the epistemic framework within which [he] constructs a notion of social "relations" that is essential for understanding the sociology of human nature' (Finlay 2007: 105). Sympathy is how we are naturally educated to share value and meaning with our social groups. The word 'sympathy' is polysemous in Hume; he uses it in at least three ways (Vitz 2004: 263–64). But he mainly uses the term to refer to a process of the

---

the hope of uncovering principles of rationality which could be applied to directing our action, Hume reversed the procedure. He began with our practice, our action, and sought to extract from it the inherent social norms.' See also Matson (2019: 33–36).

imagination by which we replicate (what we take to be) the emotional experience of others through a social transmission of impressions and ideas. The process of sympathy works as follows. We learn over time to associate various expressions and actions with different pleasant or painful passions. When we see what we take to be the effects of a passion in another person, we form an idea of that passion – we bring it home to ourselves. The result is that our 'idea is presently converted into an impression, and acquires such a degree of force [...] as to become the very passion itself' (T 2.1.11.3). The association of impressions and ideas necessary in the process of sympathy is facilitated by the natural resemblance between individuals (T 2.1.11.5).[18] I perceive myself to resemble others. My perception of the passions of another easily, by virtue of our natural human resemblance, leads me to form an idea of myself experiencing the same passion. Reflecting on the idea of experiencing a passion leads me to convert the idea into a version of the passion itself.

Sympathy in Hume is often emphasised as contagious, running insensibly from one person to another.[19] This is

---

18 Although we resemble all other people in some respects, we resemble some more than others. Hume thinks that our sympathy is greater, therefore, with people who look like us or resemble us in other salient ways. The relations of contiguity and cause and effect also influence the strength of our sympathy. Thus, for Hume we also sympathise strongly with those who are physically close to us and less strongly with those who are far off.

19 The contagious aspect of sympathy is often contrasted with the more deliberate and cognitive aspect of sympathy in Adam Smith (e.g. Khalil 2010). The differences between Hume and Smith on sympathy and related issues of moral approval are real but probably overstated (Matson et al. 2019: 692–701). Knud Haakonssen (1981: 45) explains that there are 'striking

undoubtedly an important element of his account. In one of his essays, for instance, he writes (EMPL 202):

> The human mind is of a very imitative nature; nor is it possible for any set of men to converse often together, without acquiring a similitude of manners, and communicating to each other their vices as well as virtues. The propensity to company and society is strong in all rational creatures; and the same disposition, which gives us this propensity, makes us enter deeply into each other's sentiments, and causes like passions and inclinations to run, as it were, by contagion, through the whole club or knot of companions.

The contagious element of sympathy in Hume prefigures modern analyses of mirror neurons, which lead people to mimic the behaviour and replicate the emotions of those around them (Hardin 2007: 41). The contagious nature of sympathy and its connection to desires implies that choice is affected not merely by long-run social conditioning, but by momentary frames of reference. To take an example, my decision to order or not order a certain menu item at a restaurant will depend to some extent on who I am with and how I anticipate their reaction to my intended meal choice. These contagious effects of sympathy map over

---

structural similarities between the theories of sympathy in [Smith and Hume] and that the equally striking differences come about because Smith broadens and generalizes Hume's idea'. For Hume, sympathy recreates the passion another is experiencing; for Smith, sympathy recreates the entire moral experience that gave rise to the passion. There is, therefore, a more pronounced cognitive dimension to Smith's sympathy than Hume's.

to what Thaler and Sunstein (2009: 57) call 'following the herd' – the conformity of preferences to group inclinations.

But it is also important to understand that the impact of sympathy goes beyond mirroring or contagion. We don't *just* follow the herd, according to Hume. We reflect on what our previous herds, as it were, have taught us about situations. Sympathy 'combines with beliefs reflecting custom-based general rules' (Taylor 2015: 37). That is, sympathetic experience leads us to form mental associations about the conditions and circumstances in which various passions are commonly experienced. By virtue of association with previous sympathies, we will experience passions in circumstances and in connection with objects that we believe to normally cause those passions (T 2.1.6.9). We experience passions in such a manner even if we are alone, or if those we are with show signs of different passions than we would expect (for instance, in cross-cultural experiences). By Hume's account, we should expect choice situations that 'prime' various aspects of our past and senses of identity to elicit different kinds of desires (cf. Akerlof and Kranton 2000).

In addition to its contagious, circumstantial effects, then, we can say that sympathy educates us about socially acceptable standards of behaviour, determining 'the just value of everything' and the 'proportions we ought to observe in preferring one object to another' (T 2.1.6.9). 'Just value' and 'proportions we ought to observe' here are to be understood as social phenomena: what we ought to observe is what others in our social group, from a general point of view, feel we ought to observe and what we ourselves, given the importance of the opinions of others, feel we ought to observe.[20]

With an understanding of the indirect passions and the role of sympathy in determining their objects, we can consider their connection to preferences and choice. The conceptual connection is illustrated in Figure 2.

Figure 2  The sympathetic formation of preferences

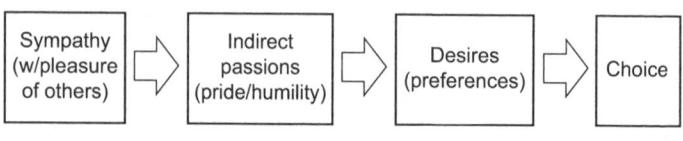

Sympathy educates our indirect passions by teaching us what other people value. Since we naturally care deeply about the feelings of others, sympathy structures our experience of the indirect passions by determining their causes. We feel proud if we are closely and uniquely associated with a quality or object that we believe pleases others. The indirect passions then affect our desires. We desire to acquire objects and develop – or at least exhibit – character traits that will make us feel proud and that will garner the love and esteem of others. We desire to disassociate

---

20 The determination of 'just value' and 'what we ought to observe' by the sentiments of qualified spectators opens the door into Hume's passionate conception of practical reason (Schafer 2008). What one ought to do is the thing which an impartial spectator, or a spectator from a general point of view, would approve of. There are, of course, myriad knowledge problems in determining what an impartial spectator would approve of in any particular situation. Such problems suggest that practical reason in a Humean sense is not amenable to precise, non-contextual rules for conduct.

with objects and rid ourselves of character traits that will humiliate us and make us the object of hatred. Hume speaks to this relationship directly (T 2.3.9.4):

> These indirect passions, being always agreeable or uneasy, give in their turn additional force to the direct passions, and encrease our desire and aversion to the object. Thus a suit of fine cloaths produces pleasure from their beauty; and this pleasure produces the direct passions, or the impressions of volition and desire. Again, when these cloaths are consider'd as belonging to ourselves, the double relation conveys to us the sentiment of pride, which is an indirect passion; and the pleasure, which attends the passion, returns back to the direct affections, and gives new force to our desire or volition, joy or hope.

The relationship illustrated in Figure 2 has implications for economic behaviour in a number of areas. One is consumption. In advanced stages of society, a major aspect of consumption behaviour is, as Thorstein Veblen (e.g. 2007: 22) would put it, 'invidious'.[21] Our preferences for consumer goods – beyond our desires for subsistence and security – are chiefly driven by interpersonal comparison. Christopher Finlay (2007: 88) emphasises the point: '[goods] become desirable to and individual within a frame of reference that involves relationships not only between

---

21 Veblen emphasises that this term is not to be understood in an evaluative sense, but rather as an assertion of matter of fact. Hume would probably prefer the term 'comparative' to 'invidious'; his contemporary Bernard Mandeville, however, would appreciate Veblen's ascription.

the self and surrounding objects but between the self and other selves, whether present at the scene of enjoyment or merely imagined.' Our demand for many particular goods hinges on our belief that they are perceived in a certain way by others, a belief that is created and sustained by sympathy as we see others react favourably to goods in various circumstances. Moreover, in line with the limitations of the causes of pride discussed above (T 2.1.6), we desire goods that will frame us in a peculiar or unique light. What is common to all people can never, on Hume's understanding, be a source of durable pride (like having merely average health); we derive pleasure from favourable comparison. Individuals will, therefore, to the extent that they perceive it to be possible, seek to rise above status quo levels and habits of consumption to differentiate themselves. Thus, Hume says, 'vanity [i.e. pride] becomes one of the principal recommendations of riches, and is the chief reason, why we either desire them for ourselves, or esteem them in others' (T 2.2.6.21).[22]

## Commerce and satisfaction in action

Embracing aspects of Hume's theory, some behavioural and institutional economists point to associated drawbacks of

---

22 It is important to note that the interpersonal nature of consumption makes it an integral part of society. It has a natural cohesive function. Consumption signals status, differentiates between class, and by extension serves as the basis of social and political stability: 'the different ranks of men,' Hume says, 'are, in great measure, regulated by riches, and that with regard to superiors as well as inferiors, strangers as well as acquaintance' (T 2.2.5.11).

commercial society. Given our susceptibility to framing through pleasant and painful associations, we might be overly prone to product persuasion. Social pressures could elicit temporary preferences that lead to bad choices – i.e. choices that run against our desire for self-control – or wasteful signaling games. Playing on the natural dynamics of sympathy and pride, new products and trends will create demand for themselves as signals or markers of social status. We may end up with an oversupply of luxury goods that are merely part of the race to the top of an endless social ladder.

Veblen provides insights along such lines, even though in a number of respects, his thought resembles Hume's.[23] Like Hume, Veblen (2007) understands wealth to have 'utility as a honorific evidence of the owner's prepotence' (21). Veblen argues that in advanced stages of society, 'those members of the community who fall short of [...] normal degree of prowess or of property suffer in the esteem of their fellow-men; and consequently they suffer also in their own esteem, since the usual basis of self-respect is the respect accorded by one's neighbours' (21). Compare Veblen's remark to Hume's comment that 'the relation, which is esteem'd the closest, and which of all others produces most commonly the passion of pride, is that of *property*' (T 2.1.10.1; italics in original).[24] Also relevant is the fact

---

23 Veblen seems to have been influenced by Hume (Edgell and Tilman 1989: 1003). In one article he refers to Hume as 'that placid unbeliever [...] not gifted with the facile acceptance of the group inheritance that made the habit of mind of his generation' (Veblen 1899: 134).

24 Hume and Veblen do, however, have very different understandings of the origin of property. For Veblen property originated from oppression. For Hume, property is a convention that extends from our sense of self;

that for Hume a considerable part of the pride produced by property relates to perceptions of social power and differentiation: 'a rich man feels the felicity of his condition better by opposing it to that of a beggar' (T 2.1.10.12).

For Veblen the invidious nature of wealth is, from the perspective of welfare, problematic – especially in commercial society. The natural productivity and dynamism of commerce means that status quo levels of consumption will fluctuate upwards. Upward dynamism implies that individuals will have to reach higher and higher levels of wealth to achieve social recognition and distinction: 'the tendency in any case is constantly to make the present pecuniary standard the point of departure for a fresh increase of wealth; and this in turn gives rise to a new standard of sufficiency and a new pecuniary classification of one's self as compared with one's neighbours' (Veblen 2007: 26). Even upon attaining status, however, individuals cannot rest contentedly. They will continually strive to increase or at least maintain their social position by further increasing their wealth. The result (Veblen 2007: 26):

> So long as the comparison is distinctly unfavourable to himself, the normal, average individual will live in chronic dissatisfaction with his present lot; and when he has reached what may be called the normal pecuniary standard of the community, or of his class in the community,

---

although it is 'artificial' (in the sense that it is not instinctive), it is 'obvious and absolutely necessary' and 'inseparable from the species' (T 3.2.1.19). For a helpful account of Hume on possession in relation to self, see Baier (1991: 135–36).

this chronic dissatisfaction will give place to a restless straining to place a wider and ever-widening pecuniary interval between himself and this average standard.

Despite his similarities to Veblen regarding the comparative essence of preferences, and his prefiguring of psychological insights from behavioural economics, Hume has a positive view of commercial society, the defining feature of which is an exchange society built on individual liberty, property and the rule of law. With the important exception of Hume's related views on public debt, he sees few drawbacks.[25] He is even more optimistic about commercial society than his friend Adam Smith, who harboured some reservations about the effects of commerce on our moral sentiments and happiness.[26] For Hume, commercial society is the form of social and economic organisation best suited for human nature. Finlay (2007: 5) says that 'Hume believed human nature to be reflected in its historically most adequate form in commercially advanced

---

25 Even his pessimism about public debt is more a comment on his views of popular government than on commerce itself: 'I am apt to think, that, in monarchical governments there is a source of improvement, and in popular governments a source of degeneracy [mortgaging public revenue], which in time will bring these species of civil government still nearer an equality' (EMPL 95). For discussion of Hume on public debt, see Paganelli (2012).

26 For a discussion of Smith's views on drawbacks of the ages of commerce, see Hanley (2009). Although Smith understands there to be problems with commercial society – one of which is that the rise of commerce can, as Veblen articulates, lead to the pursuit of *un*happiness – he still sees it as the best form of social and economic organisation and the one that is most conducive to human flourishing. For discussion of these tensions in Smith, see Matson (2021a).

contemporary European societies.' Duncan Forbes (1975: 87) notes the dependency in Hume between commerce and the good life. Neil McArthur (2007: 9) understands there to be a causal connection between the two, at least at a national level: 'commerce is the key to a nation's development towards a greater refinement and civilization.' Hume's own praise of modern commercial society comes through clearly throughout his works. Speaking to the moral effects of commerce, he claims that the ancient philosophers would think it 'incredible, the degree of humanity, clemency, order, tranquility, and other social virtues [...] attained in modern times' (EPM 7.18). Elsewhere, in what is perhaps his strongest praise of commerce (his essay 'Of Refinement in the Arts'),[27] he claims that 'the ages of refinement [i.e. the ages of commerce] are *both the happiest and the most virtuous*' (EMPL 269; italics added).

What is the connection between Hume's optimism toward commercial society and his endogenous account of preferences? Scholars have offered accounts of Hume's optimism in terms of its political and institutional effects (Schabas 2014; Wennerlind 2011; McArthur 2007); its positive effects on manners and culture (Boyd 2008); its tendency to disintegrate parochialism and promote cosmopolitanism (McArthur 2014); and its effects on intellectual freedom (Merrill 2015a: 149). But what I would like to emphasise is in some respects a more fundamental issue relating to Hume's ideas about happiness. Whereas happiness or well-being is understood, or at least assumed,

---

[27] This essay was originally published under the title 'Of Luxury'.

in much of economic thought to be a matter of preference satisfaction, Hume takes it to largely reside in the process of pursuing and developing preferences. He theorises that it is often not the satisfaction of desires themselves that fundamentally concern us; it is the having and the pursuing of desires. Whereas for Veblen and others commercial society might lead to perennial dissatisfaction as individuals strive but never quite satisfy their desire for personal distinction and rank, Hume sees such striving as satisfying the mind's natural desire for action and purpose.

In 'Of Refinement in the Arts' Hume says that 'human happiness, according to the most received notions, seems to consist in three ingredients; action, pleasure, and indolence' (EMPL 269).[28] He takes action as the pursuit of a pleasurable end. Pleasure is simply enjoyment itself. Indolence derives its value instrumentally from action and pleasure by helping the mind rest and prepare for future action and pleasure. From Hume's statement on happiness and the surrounding text in 'Of Refinement in the Arts', Eugene Rotwein (2009: xxxvi) distils three distinct 'causes of labor': (1) the desire for pleasure, (2) the desire for action and (3) the desire for liveliness. The desire for pleasure basically overlaps with the above account of preferences. The desire for action reflects our desire to be engaged in pursuit of pleasurable, meaningful ends. The final desire, the desire for liveliness, is our desire for desires. As Rotwein

---

28 These 'received notions', it turns out, map over quite nicely to his four essays – 'The Epicurean', 'The Stoic', 'The Platonist' and 'The Sceptic' – that together comprise an interesting dialogue on the nature of happiness (Immerwahr 1989).

(2009) describes this last desire, 'economic behavior [for Hume] involves not merely a desire for want-gratification but further reflects a desire to *have* and *pursue* wants' (xlvii; italics in original).

Satisfying our desire for enjoyment, i.e. satisfying our preferences, is a relatively small part of our happiness. Hume indicates in a number of places that satisfying the desires for action and liveliness are more important.[29] He maintains that in addition to our disposition for reflection and socialisation, we are constituted for action. 'Man is an active being; and from that disposition, as well as from the various necessities of human life, must submit to business and occupation' (EHU 1.6). In line with our active disposition, we crave purposeful employment for its own sake. He says in 'Of Interest', 'There is no craving or demand of the human mind more constant and insatiable than that for exercise and employment; this desire seems the foundation of most of our passions and pursuits' (EMPL 300). In 'The Stoic', he similarly asserts – albeit not technically in his own voice – that 'labour itself is the chief ingredient of the felicity to which thou aspires, and that every enjoyment soon becomes insipid and distasteful, when not acquired by fatigue and industry' (EMPL 149).

In addition to the fact that we desire action as such, the satisfaction in action eclipses the satisfaction in the ends of action. Hume elaborates in the concluding section of Book 2 of the *Treatise*, 'Of Curiosity or the Love of Truth' (T 2.3.10). He begins there by discussing the motivation to

---

[29] This paragraph and the next draw from Rotwein (2009).

philosophy. We are generally more interested in the process of solving intellectual puzzles than in the usefulness of the solutions considered independently. The truth that philosophers attempt to discover must be perceived to have some usefulness; but that usefulness itself is second-hand to the pleasure of inquiry: 'If the importance of the truth be requisite to compleat the pleasure, 'tis not on account of any considerable enjoyment, but only because 'tis, in some measure, requisite to fix our attention' (T 2.3.10.6). He goes on to compare philosophy to hunting – another activity often pursued for the activity itself, not for its ends. As with philosophy, the usefulness of the ends is really incidental. It is simply required to fix the imagination: 'A man of the greatest fortune, and the farthest remov'd from avarice, tho' he takes pleasure in hunting after partridges and pheasants, feels no satisfaction in shooting crows and magpies; and that because he considers the first as fit for the table, and the other as entirely useless' (T 2.3.10.8). The chief satisfaction comes from the hunt, not from the prey itself. The usefulness or suitability of the prey is merely required to confer pleasure back on the activity, to give it purpose.

The importance of action over pleasure, process over ends, is not confined to philosophy and hunting. It is an important feature of human nature more broadly, with important applications in economic contexts. The desire for action and liveliness underlies Hume's famous description of the psychology of accumulation: 'if the employment you give [a man] be lucrative, especially if the profit be attached to a particular exertion of industry, he has gain so often in his eye, that he acquires, by degrees, a passion for it, and knows no such pleasure as that of seeing the daily increase of his fortune' (EMPL 301). Note that this passage immediately follows Hume's claim that 'there is no craving [...] of the human mind more constant and insatiable than that for exercise and employment' (EMPL 300). One interpretation of Hume's psychology of accumulation then is that individuals desire action toward meaningful ends and a perpetuation of desire, and that those desires are honourably gratified in commercial enterprise. The ends of enterprise – fortune and social status – are important for fixing the imagination and conferring meaning onto our pursuits. But we are largely interested in the process itself.

The expression of the desire for action and liveliness depends crucially on the perceived potential scope of purposeful activities. This then is the connection between Hume's account of preferences and his optimism about commercial society: he interprets the freedom and dynamism that commerce naturally brings as increasing opportunity and providing an array of new purposes (including social distinction) that serve as an outlet for the desire for action and thereby contribute to happiness.

There is support for such an interpretation in the conjectural history that Hume sketches in the first two essays of his *Political Discourses*, 'Of Commerce' and 'Of Refinement in the Arts'.[30] Hume says that in the ages of agriculture,

---

30 Hume's *Political Discourses* are a subset of his *Essays, Moral, Political, and Literary*. The *Political Discourses* were first published in 1752. The *Political Discourses* comprised the most successful volume of Hume's *Essays*, with a second and third edition published in 1752 and 1754 (see Miller 1987: xi–xviii). The essays within the 1754 edition of *Political Discourses* are:

'where manufactures and mechanic arts are not cultivated,' individuals have no incentive to apply themselves to produce what is needed beyond their subsistence. Indolence prevails in that individuals 'cannot exchange [their] superfluity for any commodities, which may serve either to their pleasure or vanity' (EMPL 261). The introduction of foreign exchange provides individuals with the opportunity to trade for new goods. They begin producing above subsistence levels and export their produce. At least in the case of England, foreign luxury wares appear on the scene, which become desirable for their pleasure and function as markers of status. Hume says, 'this perhaps is the chief advantage which arises from a commerce with strangers. It rouses men from their indolence; and presenting the gayer and more opulent part of the nation with objects of luxury, which they never before dreamed of, raises in them a desire of a more splendid way of life than what their ancestors enjoyed' (EMPL 264). He therefore frames the chief advantage of commerce as lying not in its material effects, but in the array of feasible opportunities it presents to the imagination. Commerce gives individuals 'as their reward, the occupation itself, as well as those pleasures which are the fruit of their labour' (EMPL 270).

The active mindset that commerce instigates does not confine itself to production and exchange. It spills over

---

(1) 'Of Commerce'; (2) 'Of Refinement in the Arts'; (3) 'Of Money'; (4) 'Of Interest'; (5) 'Of the Balance of Trade'; (6) 'Of the Balance of Power'; (7) 'Of Taxes'; (8) 'Of Public Credit'; (9) 'Of some Remarkable Customs'; (10) 'Of the Populousness of Ancient Nations'; (11) 'Of the Protestant Succession'; and (12) 'Idea of a Perfect Commonwealth.'

into the liberal arts, giving the mind outlets in natural and moral sciences, including politics and ethics. 'The spirit of the age affects all the arts; and the minds of men, being once roused from their lethargy, and put into fermentation, turn themselves on all sides, and carry improvements into every art and science' (EMPL 271). In one of his best-known passages, Hume famously illustrates his view of the commercial stage in history (EMPL 271; italics in original):

> The more these refined arts [both liberal and mechanical arts] advance, the more sociable men become: nor is it possible, that, when enriched with science, and possessed of a fund of conversation, they should be contented to remain in solitude, or live with their fellow-citizens in that distant manner, which is peculiar to ignorant and barbarous nations. They flock into cities; love to receive and communicate knowledge; to show their wit or their breeding; their taste in conversation or living, in clothes or furniture. Particular clubs and societies are everywhere formed: Both sexes meet in an easy and sociable manner; and the tempers of men, as well as their behavior, refine apace. So that, beside the improvements which they receive from knowledge and the liberal arts, it is impossible but they must feel an increase of humanity, from the very habit of conversing together, and contributing to each other's pleasure and entertainment. Thus *industry*, *knowledge*, and *humanity*, are linked together by an indissoluble chain, and are found, from experience as well as reason, to be peculiar to the more polished, and, what are commonly denominated, the more luxurious ages.

Hume sees the intrapersonal desire for refinement and social virtue to be an important consequence of commerce. This consequence is normally treated in terms of its humanising effects, i.e. in terms of its tendency to increase benevolence through the dovetailing of interests and the increase in social interaction (e.g. McArthur 2014). But it might also be interpreted in terms of the desire for action and liveliness. Self-refinement, taken as a desire to be perceived as virtuous relative to one's social group, gives the mind a focus – it constitutes a demand for personal improvement, a demand to cultivate what Hume elsewhere calls a 'delicacy of taste' (EMPL: 3–8). The desire for self-refinement is naturally bolstered as one's social experience diversifies and broadens. Commerce not only instigates such diversification, but also provides means for social and class mobility by which individuals transcend their present state. Self-refinement features as part of a broader desire for sympathetic pleasure and status. In sociological terms, the key here for Hume is the fact that commerce introduces a new social class that gains honour and respectability, not on the basis of heritage, but through accumulating wealth: 'peasants, by a proper cultivation of the land, become rich and independent; while the tradesmen and merchants acquire a share of the property, and draw authority and consideration to that middling rank of men' (EMPL 277). Class effects are important in that they change the array of the possible, giving purpose and pleasure in the pursuits of both character and wealth, which again are in large part sought for their social and comparative effects.

## Conclusion

Given Hume's psychological sophistication (Reed and Vitz 2018) and his affinities to recent work in behavioural economics (e.g. Palacious-Huerta 2003; Sugden 2006), his ideas in economic philosophy, which are connected to his psychology, warrant attention. As I've argued, he holds that preferences are largely comparative desires created through interpersonal sympathetic processes. This understanding helps to explain his optimism about commercial society because he interprets the having, the pursuing and the transforming of desires to be an essential part of wellbeing. We want to have wants; we derive pleasure from aspiration and occupation. His thought in these respects resembles Frank Knight (1922: 458), who maintains that 'the chief thing which the common-sense individual actually wants is not satisfactions for the wants which he has, but more and *better* wants' (italics in original).[31] Hume might slightly qualify Knight's point and note that the extent to which one desires higher wants – i.e. the dynamism of preferences themselves – depends on the scope of perceived opportunity: 'Banish those arts [mechanical] from society, you deprive men both of action and pleasure; and leaving nothing but indolence in their place, you even destroy the relish of indolence' (EMPL 270).

In any case, like Knight, Hume's thought may be appropriately seen as a challenge to ideas that welfare should be

---

31 Hume's emphasis on the human desire for play and gaming at T 2.3.10 also anticipates Knight (1923).

conceived strictly in terms of preference satisfaction. That challenge extends to the policy recommendations from behavioural welfare economics, many of which assume that the human goal is preference satisfaction (Dold and Rizzo 2021). Hume's thought provides a basis for challenging the welfare criterion and associated public policies one finds in much of behavioural welfare economics (cf. Sugden 2021). The human goal is not simply satisfaction, but also action – the pursuit and refinement of desires, not just desires in and of themselves.

# 4 THE BEHAVIOURAL ECONOMIST IN SOCIETY

> Do you come to the philosopher as to a *cunning man*, to learn something by magic or witchcraft, beyond what can be known by common prudence and discretion? – Yes; we come to a philosopher to be instructed, how we shall chuse our ends, more than the means for attaining these ends: We want to know what desire we shall gratify, what passion we shall comply with, what appetite we shall indulge ...
>
> I am very sorry then, I have pretended to be a philosopher.
>
> — *The Sceptic* (Hume 1994: 161; italics in original)

In *Escaping Paternalism*, Mario Rizzo and Glen Whitman (Rizzo and Whitman 2020; hereafter cited as 'RW') criticise behavioural paternalists for relying on a standard of welfare derived from the neoclassical model of rationality. According to that standard, welfare consists in the satisfaction of one's true preferences, which are conceived as context-independent and representable as a complete and transitive ranking of choice options. There is little empirical evidence, according to Rizzo and Whitman, that individuals have true preferences of that sort (cf. Infante et al. 2016). Behavioural paternalists simply tend to 'assume that *there must be a well-defined answer* to what is in someone's best interests, which we can discern if we just look hard enough' (RW: 400; italics in original). In doing so, they 'substitute their own judgments rather than confront the indeterminacy in the data' (RW: 401).

Against behavioural paternalism Rizzo and Whitman defend a concept of inclusive rationality: 'Inclusive rationality means purposeful behavior based on subjective preferences and beliefs, in the presence of both environmental and cognitive constraints' (RW: 26). Their conception of inclusive rationality implies an open-ended conception of welfare under which individuals purposefully pursue their own good as they understand it, in the way they see fit. Welfare need not be conceived as satisfying a set of complete and transitive (i.e. 'true') preferences. Indeed, temporary inconsistency or a certain amount of preference rotation might simply illustrate what John Stuart Mill called 'experiments in living' (2003: 122). Rizzo and Whitman elaborate: 'No such thing as "welfare" exists until an individual mind comes into being ... The human mind determines what is good for itself. It seems incredibly peculiar, at best, to support a standard of the mind's well-being that may be rejected (indeed, often *is rejected*) by the mind itself' (RW: 406; italics in original).

In response to the conceptual difficulties and moralistic dangers that Rizzo and Whitman perceive to be inherent in the behavioural paternalist project, they outline at the end of their book 'a better path forward' (RW: 437). Drawing on Mill's Harm Principle, they argue that we should abstain from coercion, even if we believe that coercion will improve individuals' happiness. Mill also says, however, that if we believe that some choices or ways of living will make an individual happier, then we have 'good reasons for remonstrating with him, or reasoning with him, or persuading him, or entreating him' (quoted in RW: 437). Following Mill, Rizzo and Whitman argue that behavioural economists should take on the role of friendly advisors, contributors to a body of helpful advice for life improvement. Behavioural economists ought to provide 'potentially useful information and perspective' and be 'friendly voices offering helpful suggestions for better living' (RW: 438). The behavioural economist should approach her fellow citizens not as one condescending from enlightenment, but as a fellow traveller proffering her ideas about the path towards happiness.

The present essay looks to extend Rizzo and Whitman's ideas about welfare, preferences and the proper role of the behavioural welfare economist in society through a consideration of the ideas of David Hume. Beyond the fact that he anticipates findings of behavioural economics (see comments in the introductory remarks to this volume), Hume is of interest in the present context because, as sketched in the previous chapter, he integrates his psychological insights on human nature into a larger moral project. He integrates his study of the mind into a wider consideration of 'men as united in society, and dependent on each other' (Hume 2007: 407) – a study of political economy. It is in this integration that we see Hume's continuing relevance for contemporary debates in behavioural welfare economics; it is to this integration that we turn for support and extension of key aspects of Rizzo and Whitman's critique of the new paternalism.

We discuss four points of contact between Hume and Rizzo and Whitman's ideas. (1) Like Rizzo and Whitman, who state that 'the mind's determination of what is good for itself is an ongoing process' (RW: 406), Hume holds welfare to be an open-ended phenomenon. The philosopher or political economist cannot define welfare in a one-size-fits-all fashion; she has no privileged insight into the good. There are, according to Hume, potentially many different good lives to be lived and good paths to be followed. (2) Given the open-endedness of welfare, Hume turns much of his intellectual energy towards securing a stable political framework in which individuals have the liberty and security to pursue their own welfare as they see fit, and to engage with others through voluntary association to refine their own sense of the good. The political dimension of Hume's treatment of welfare dovetails with Rizzo and Whitman's call to take up a 'paternalism-resisting framework' (RW: 434). (3) Although Hume recognises that there is a multiplicity of potential good lives, he offers some generalised insights on welfare in light of his own reflections on human nature. His reflections support aspects of Rizzo and Whitman's sensibilities on preference formation which for them is an experiential process of 'seeking to better achieve one's subjective goals and values' (RW: 438). Prefiguring ideas later developed by Frank Knight and James Buchanan (Knight 1922; Buchanan

1979), Hume suggests that a chief component of human happiness lies in the refinement of one's preferences through social engagement and the pursuit of virtue: happiness lies in the direction of self-development and discovery. (4) Finally, we argue that Hume exemplifies Rizzo and Whitman's advice to behavioural economists to approach the public as fellow-citizens or equals 'offering friendly advice' (RW: 439) rather than as enlightened elites or superiors. Following the practice of public luminaries such as Joseph Addison and Richard Steele, Hume thought that the philosopher (or the political economist) ought to view herself as a coequal participant in a public conversation, a conversation aimed at mutual personal improvement and cultural reform. Hume's vision of the public role and posture of the philosopher has relevant implications for how we think about the role of contemporary behavioural welfare economists in society.

## Dialoguing about happiness

Hume's insights on welfare come forth in his discussions on happiness. Happiness is now sometimes distinguished from well-being.[1] The word 'happiness' can be taken to mean a transitory emotional state rather than a life well lived. But happiness for Hume hearkens back to the Greek notion of *eudaimonia*, a conception of human flourishing that corresponds to modern talk of well-being (Deci and Ryan 2008). A concern for happiness in the eudemonistic

---

[1] For a helpful introduction on the modern distinction between happiness and well-being, see Haybron (2011). Throughout this essay we use the terms 'happiness', 'well-being', 'welfare' and 'flourishing' interchangeably.

sense lies at the heart of Hume's intellectual project. He understands 'human flourishing [to be] the proper aim not only of ethical precept but also of descriptive psychology' (Potkay 2000: 12).

What facilitates human flourishing? In what particular way of living does happiness consist? Hume's answer is not straightforward. He presents his perspectives on the matter dialogically in a series of four essays, first published in 1742. They are titled: 'The Epicurean', 'The Stoic', 'The Platonist' and 'The Sceptic'. In a footnote at the beginning of the first of the essays, 'The Epicurean', Hume (1994: 139) lays out the purpose of the essays:

> The intention of this and the three following essays is not so much to explain accurately the sentiments of the ancient sects of philosophy, as to deliver the sentiments of sects, that naturally form themselves in the world, and entertain different ideas of human life and of happiness. I have given each of them the name of the philosophical sect, to which it bears the greatest affinity.

The decision to treat the nature of happiness or human flourishing through four monologues – which when read together comprise a kind of dialogue – is significant. The rhetorical form of the essays, which seems to follow the lines of Cicero's *De Finibus* (Heydt 2007: 7), has a didactic purpose.[2] The multivocal form draws the reader into

---

[2] On the connection between the literary form and purpose of the happiness essays, see also Immerwahr (1989).

differing perspectives, making it clear that humans naturally have varying conceptions of the good life. The presence of different and sometimes incommensurable points of view on human flourishing among people suggests that we adopt a 'sceptically-tinged eclecticism' (Heydt 2007: 13). We should avoid dogmatically imposing our commitments upon others given that there is no single philosophical school or outlook that can provide us with final, demonstratively certain answers about the good.

The open-endedness of happiness is reinforced by the fact that perspectives from different essays dovetail with aspects of Hume's own thought.[3] In some respects we might say that Hume is the ultimate 'sceptically-tinged eclectic,' not only by virtue of his skepticism (for which he is well-known), but also by his eclecticism. The character in the first of the four essays, the Epicurean, whom Hume dubs 'the man of elegance and pleasure' (Hume 1994: 138, n. 1), takes happiness to lie in natural pleasures and the gratification of the senses. It is through the enjoyment of pleasure that we flourish as human beings. The Epicurean says to his interlocuter: 'You pretend to make me happy by reason, and by rules of art. You must, then, create me anew by rules of art. For on my original frame and structure does my happiness depend' (Hume 1994: 139). The Epicurean believes happiness to be a function of satisfying natural desire, which reason cannot hope to modify: 'When by my will alone I can stop the blood, as it runs with impetuosity along its canals, then may I hope to change the course of

---

3 This paragraph draws on Immerwahr (1989: 310–13).

my sentiments and passions' (Hume 1994: 140). The course of human happiness is evident in our passions themselves. There is not much more to be said on the matter: 'why do I apply to you, proud and ignorant sages, to shew me the road to happiness? Let me consult my own passions and inclinations. In them must I read the dictates of nature; not in your frivolous discourses' (Hume 1994: 141). Such points of view echo Hume's own comments throughout his work on the relation between reason and the passions (Hume 2007: 266) and on the satisfaction of refined pleasures.[4]

The next character of the essays, the Stoic, is dubbed 'the man of action and virtue' (Hume 1994: 146). He writes in response to the Epicurean. Happiness for the Stoic is furthered not as we simply satisfy our passions, but as we pursue art and industry, as we cultivate virtue and society. The Stoic conceives of happiness as essentially dynamic, not static. Happiness lies in the pursuit and the constant transformation or development of desires, not simply in the satisfaction of desires themselves (Hume 1994: 149). Hume's own perspective, which we can distinguish from the perspective of any of the four happiness essays alone, has the most in common with the Stoic (Livingston 1998:

---

[4] For an insightful interpretation of Hume as a qualified kind of Epicurean, see Dorsey (2015). There is much to be said for Dorsey's interpretation of Hume as accepting a 'unique hybrid of hedonism and *perfectionism*: a view that indexes the value of individual pleasures to the extent to which these pleasures conform to, or are fitting of, a particularly sentimentalist conception of human nature' (p. 246; italics in original). Dorsey, however, seems to miss the fact that a significant part of human happiness for Hume lies in its *pursuit*, not strictly in the satisfaction, of desires (Rotwein 2009: xlvii; Potkay 2000: 69; see also the previous chapter).

138; Walker 2013). We return to the Stoic below. For now, it is useful to note that the conception of happiness as dynamic is significant for Hume's political economy (e.g. Hume 1994: 270–71; Rotwein 2009: xlvii). The dynamic element of happiness has implications for contemporary discussions. In the context of behavioural welfare economics, the dynamic conception of happiness points out that welfare might *not* consist in a stable, time-consistent set of preferences, but in the activity of pursuing one's desires and even transforming them into something new. The main argument in one's utility function, so to speak, might paradoxically be the redefining of one's utility function, the discovering and the cultivating of better taste.

The Platonist, dubbed 'the man of contemplation and *philosophical* devotion' (Hume 1994: 155, n. 1; italics in original), presents the perspective with which Hume appears to sympathise least. 'The Platonist' is the shortest of the four essays. The essay arrives at the point that humans undermine their own well-being when they focus on 'sensual pleasure or popular applause'; this is because humans are 'made for the contemplation of the Supreme Being, and of his works' (Hume 1994: 156). It is in the contemplation of the divine and the ideal that happiness lies.

The character of the final and most probing essay is the Sceptic. The Sceptic has sometimes been taken to represent Hume's own position and as undermining the opinions expressed by the Epicurean, the Stoic and the Platonist (e.g. Fogelin 1985: 117–19; cf. Immerwahr 1989). The arguments of the Sceptic are best understood, however, not as totally undermining the positions of the previous essays but as providing a critical framework within which the activity of philosophising about happiness ought to take place. 'The speech of the "Sceptic" is not merely another speech about happiness. It is also and primarily a speech about the limits of philosophical theories of happiness' (Livingston 1998: 98). Whereas the Epicurean, the Stoic and the Platonist consider the question, 'what is human happiness?', the Sceptic, while offering some modest insights about happiness, is primarily concerned with the question, 'what can *philosophers* hope to say about human happiness?'

The perspective conveyed by the Sceptic relates to Hume's dialectical conception of philosophy (Livingston 1984; Merrill 2015a: 153–60; cf. Stewart 1991) and the faculty of reason in particular (Matson 2017). What is philosophy, and what can the philosopher hope to accomplish? Hume discovers that the philosopher cannot hope to extricate herself from a web of pre-philosophical beliefs, habits and feelings. These beliefs, habits and feelings constitute the basic faculties by which philosophical reasoning is undertaken (e.g. our causal inferences, our belief in a world of external objects, our reliance on probabilistic reasoning, etc.). Hume's reflection on these matters leads him to invert the early modern (Cartesian, Lockean) trend in epistemology. His philosophy, as it progresses, moves from a perspective of 'I Think' to a social one of 'We Do' (Capaldi 1989: 22):

> Instead of attempting to scrutinize our thought process in the hope of uncovering principles of rationality which could be applied to directing our action, Hume reversed

> the procedure. He began with our practice, our action, and sought to extract from it the inherent social norms.

In other words, Hume understands philosophy to be an immanent practice from within the common course of human affairs by which the philosopher attempts to reconstruct partial bits of life as it is lived and observed. The philosopher with proper self-knowledge and cognizance of the limits of the philosophic enterprise turns from foundational metaphysical issues, which involve questions that human reason cannot hope to resolve, to matters of morals, politics and aesthetics, about which we might develop a 'set of opinions, which if not true (for that, perhaps, is too much to be hoped for) might at least be satisfactory to the human mind' (Hume 2007: 177).

Hume's view of philosophy, as communicated through the Sceptic, has important implications for his politics (Danford 1990; Livingston 1998; Merrill 2015a) and his political economy (Matson 2019). What does it have to do with happiness? Simply this: when giving policy advice, the philosopher cannot hope to rise above the insights of common ways of thinking to provide us with a definitive set of answers to questions about the good life. Although we might be able to 'speak of what happiness is in the light of the natures we ourselves have' (Merrill 2015a: 157), when thinking about policies and legislation, we need to candidly recognise that there may well be more than one pathway to happiness. We can find 'no absolute obligations or imperatives' (Merrill 2015a: 157) for institutional design in the course of nature, only common maxims, inherited traditions and prudential recommendations.

As indicated by the epigraph of this essay, politicians and citizens ought not look to the philosopher – or the behavioural economist – as a *'cunning man'* (an eighteenth-century phrase for magician) capable of pointing them towards the good life. Indeed, in their discourse on the good life, Hume remarks, the opinions of philosophers ought to be subject to a higher-than-normal level of scrutiny: philosophers 'confine too much their principles, and make no account of that vast variety, which nature has so much affected in all her operations' (Hume 1994: 159); 'they are led astray, not only by the narrowness of their understandings, but by that also of their passions ... it is difficult for [them] to apprehend, that any thing, which appears totally indifferent to [them], can ever give enjoyment to any other person' (Hume 1994: 160). In other words, philosophers are often guilty of imposing their own vision of happiness on others.[5] The Sceptic is pointing out that the Epicurean, the Stoic and the Platonist have assumed that others are as they are, and find enjoyment and fulfilment as they do. We think that Hume's indictment applies, in some instances, to new paternalists, who, in arguing for the existence of true preferences, seem to believe that those preferences align with 'folk wisdom' (RW: 400) or with what they themselves would prefer (e.g. less smoking, less sugar, more exercise, more savings). Rizzo and Whitman

---

5 As Thomas Merrill (2015a: 159) nicely puts the point, 'In their zeal to offer theoretical accounts of nature, it seems, the philosophers overlooked themselves'.

rightly refer to this as a great non sequitur (RW: 401). To the paternalists, The Sceptic rejoins (Hume 1994: 160):

> Do they not see the vast variety of inclinations and pursuits among our species; where each man seems fully satisfied with his own course of life, and would esteem it the greatest unhappiness to be confined to that of his neighbor?

## The political implications of Hume's happiness essays

Rizzo and Whitman argue that we should adopt a 'paternalism-resisting framework' (RW: 434) in public policy given behavioural economists' one-sided focus on human error-proneness and the slippery-slope problems posed by behavioural paternalist policies (see RW: 349–97). Their alternative framework does 'not begin by seeking evidence of errors, but by seeking understanding' (RW: 434):

> A paternalism-resisting framework would ... take a more permissive attitude toward preferences that appear inconsistent and incomplete, and would then ask how people with such nonstandard preferences would approach the world. That inquiry naturally leads to exploration of people's diverse and idiosyncratic strategies of self-management, as well as how markets, families, clubs, and other voluntary associations can assist in the process.

The implicit political logic of the 'paternalism-resisting framework' is essentially the logic of classical liberal political thought of, for instance, Locke, Hume and Smith, and Mill. On that logic our general presumption should be that people are reasonable beings, cultivating and pursuing their values as they see fit. Given an inclusive understanding of rationality and welfare, our political efforts ought to be largely focused on securing a framework of stable rules within which individuals can peaceably live their lives. There is reason to think that such a message is an unspoken but important implication of Hume's happiness essays (Harris 2007; Merrill 2015a: 150–61).

Across the happiness essays Hume illustrates the natural diversity of human preferences and perspectives. Different perspectives on happiness may be especially divergent, such as the perspectives of the Epicurean and the Platonist. Members of various philosophical sects may find it difficult to find common ground for discussion; perspectives on the good life might to a large extent be incommensurable. The natural political implication of Hume's perspective is that we should shift our focus in politics, as much as we can, from considering and pursuing substantive ends towards considering and pursuing effective means that enable peaceful coexistence among individuals with different ends. In the pluralism of the modern world, it is important to respect one another's passions and goals, and seek a frame of rules that enables each of us, as much as possible, to pursue our own ends. Attempts to build a political consensus around any one theory of the good may lead to open violence and oppression.

Attempts to join politics with theories of the good in the early modern era led to a particularly dangerous fusion of politics and religion (Hume 1994: 73–79). That fusion resulted in a great deal of violence in the seventeenth and eighteenth centuries. When Hume wrote his happiness essays in the 1740s, 'the memories of the St. Bartholomew's Day Massacre, of the sack of Magdeburg in the Thirty Years' War, of the Revocation of the Edict of Nantes, among others, were still within reach' (Merrill 2015b: 31). In light of the danger of joining religion and politics – and speculative philosophy and politics more generally (Hume 1994: 54–63; Livingston 1984: 8) – Hume understood the public role of the philosopher to be that of providing a calming, analytical perspective on partisan positions to facilitate agreement about the essential goals of a political order (Immerwahr 1992; Asher 2021). Philosophy (Hume 2000: 8),

> if carefully cultivated by several, must gradually diffuse itself throughout the whole society, and bestow a similar correctness on every art and calling. The politician will acquire greater foresight and subtilty, in the dividing and balancing of power ... the stability of modern governments ... will still improve, by similar gradations.[6]

The improvement Hume speaks of comes as individuals within the polity are able to turn away from partisan theories of the good and work to shore up what we can call 'constitutional conventions' (cf. Sabl 2012: 32–34). Generally speaking, 'conventions' in Hume are practices that each individual citizen finds in his or her interest

---

6  For discussion, see Whelan (1985: 330).

to adopt, provided that he or she expects the majority of other citizens to adopt them.[7] Hume uses his concept of convention to explain a wide range of social phenomena from language and money to gallantry, norms of chastity, and the rules of traffic (Hardin 2007: 85).[8] Constitutional conventions are practices that individuals find in their mutual interest, without which extended social life beyond the family would not be possible.[9] Such conventions are 'constitutional' because they constitute the basic structure of the polity. The most fundamental of these conventions are the rules of possession, transference by consent, and contract. Hume calls these conventions 'the laws of nature'; they are everywhere inseparable from human society (Hume 2007: 311). In service to these conventions are

---

[7] Hume's theory of convention prefigures and can usefully be interpreted in light of the theory of David K. Lewis (1969). For discussion, see, for example, Vanderschraaf (1998), Hardin (2007: 83) and Matson and Klein (2022); cf. Barry (2010).

[8] Humean conventions have a flavour of what game theorists call coordination games. With traffic, for instance, it doesn't particularly matter to us whether we drive on the right or left; what matters is that we arrive at a mutual understanding (a convention) with others such that we always drive on the same side.

[9] Constitutional conventions, therefore, cannot entirely be captured by the logic of games of pure coordination. In so far as they are necessary for extended social life, in some respect they are not 'conventional' at all. Without *some* rudiments of justice, for instance, society would cease to exist. Yet constitutional conventions do have a genuinely conventional element. The existence of *a* political authority is not really 'conventional' in that there is no alternative other than the crumbling of society. But the particular *type* of political authority is conventional in that there are multiple alternatives (political regimes; particular individuals to empower) around which individuals can coordinate. For discussion, see Matson and Klein (2022). See also Binmore (2005: 48).

conventions of political authority and allegiance. Political regimes warrant our support and allegiance insofar as they preserve and reinforce the rules of property, which allow for peaceable coexistence, voluntary association and individual pursuits within the rule of law. Political orders, whatever their particular origin, warrant allegiance insofar as they preserve liberty, which is 'the perfection of civil society' (Hume 1994: 41). Our political economy should be built upon, and primarily concerned with reinforcing, our society's constitutional conventions given the lack of consensus around and about the higher good.

## Hume's qualified theory of happiness

Although he doesn't think that we can conclude definitively what happiness is, Hume thinks it is nonetheless meaningful to discuss happiness in light of our personal understanding and assessments of human nature (Merrill 2015a: 157). There is much in Hume's own understanding of happiness to corroborate Rizzo and Whitman's inclusive, process-oriented view of rationality and welfare. For Rizzo and Whitman rationality and welfare-improving choices are 'the result of a dialectical process in which the reasoner approaches an issue first from one perspective, then from another, and so on for perhaps many stages' (Rizzo and Whitman 2018: 209).

We maintain that Hume's perspective on happiness prefigures that of the 'Old Chicago' political economists, e.g. Frank Knight (1922) and James Buchanan (1979), who interpret welfare in broadly dynamic terms (Dold and

Rizzo 2021; Lewis and Dold 2020). Welfare is not, on such an understanding, simply a matter of satisfying a static, well-ordered array of preferences. Welfare involves creating and refining preferences. That understanding is important in Hume.

Dynamic ideas about happiness come forth across Hume's work. They are, as we've mentioned, pronounced in the essay 'The Stoic'. Donald Livingston notes that 'Hume's own view of human excellence is expressed in "The Stoic"', and that 'the task of "The Sceptic" is to disentangle the speech of the Stoic from the false philosophy in which it is embedded' (Livingston 1998: 138).[10] Put differently, Hume largely sympathises with the Stoic, but qualifies his sympathies by communicating through the Sceptic that even his own views are not to be taken as sacrosanct.

Describing the view of happiness conveyed in 'The Stoic', Adam Potkay notes that 'our happiness is such that our endeavors toward it largely compose it' (Potkay 2000: 69). Throughout 'The Stoic', Hume points out that it is in action and industry that our well-being principally lies. The belief that simply satisfying our desires will satisfy us is largely an illusion. Rest and the indulgence of pleasure 'becomes a fatigue'; 'the mind, unexercised, finds every delight insipid and loathsome' (Hume 1994: 150). We do, of course, desire pleasure. But over the desire for pleasure itself, our mind

---

10  The limited comments on the nature of happiness that Hume communicates in 'The Sceptic' broadly parallel the themes in 'The Stoic'. In his famous essay 'Of Refinement in the Arts' Hume maintains that 'human happiness, according to the most received notions, seems to consist in three ingredients; action, pleasure, and indolence' (Hume 1994: 269). Cf. Walker (2013).

has a desire for the *pursuit* of pleasure: 'there is no craving or demand of the human mind more constant and insatiable than that for exercise and employment; this desire seems the foundation of most of our passions and pursuits' (Hume 1994: 300). Our interest in most activities derives only very indirectly from the pleasure or utility of the ends of those activities. The usefulness of the ends is only required to 'fix our attention' (Hume 2007: 288); usefulness in the ends that we pursue is chiefly valued for the meaning that it confers on the pursuit of our ends, including the fulfilment when those pursuits meet with some success. In his *Treatise* Hume illustrates the point with a hunting example: 'a man of the greatest fortune, and the farthest removed from avarice, tho' he takes pleasure in hunting after partridges and pheasants, feels no satisfaction in shooting crows and magpies; and that because he considers the first as fit for the table, and the other as entirely useless' (Hume 2007: 288). There is an interplay between the usefulness of ends and the enjoyment of the pursuit: the hunter mainly enjoys the hunt itself; but the hunt is enjoyable only if there is *some* value in the prey.

Beyond the desire for action, however, the human mind – at least as it develops through social interaction in modern commercial societies[11] – naturally desires 'liveliness', which, as Eugene Rotwein describes it, 'reflects a desire to *have* and *pursue* wants' (Rotwein 2009: xlvii; italics in

---

11 Hume notes that the desire for self-refinement in part depends on one's perceived scope of opportunity and cultural context: 'Banish those arts [of commerce] from society, you deprive men of both action and pleasure; and leaving nothing but indolence in their place, you destroy even the relish of indolence' (Hume 1994: 270).

original). Hume's ideas about our desire for liveliness correspond to a point emphasised by Knight: 'Life is not fundamentally a striving for ends, for satisfactions, but rather for bases for further striving; desire is more fundamental to conduct than is achievement, or perhaps better, the true achievement is the refinement and elevation of the plane of desire, the cultivation of taste' (Knight 1922: 459). The desire for liveliness is an outflow of human creativity and innovation. Our creative faculties are perhaps initially developed through external application: through art and physical industry, through exchange and the creation of value. But the mind naturally turns upon itself. *We* are our own greatest undertaking: 'thou thyself shouldest also be the object of thy industry, and that by art and attention alone thou canst acquire that ability, which will raise thee to the proper station in the universe' (Hume 1994: 147). The mind is the ultimate resource; the cultivation of the mind is the ultimate end towards which that resource is put.[12]

## Philosophy as a scene of conversation

The methodological and rhetorical implications of Hume's happiness essays, along with the historical way in which Hume and other eighteenth-century Britons came to

---

12 For ideas about self-refinement in Hume, see his essays on taste, 'Of the Delicacy of Taste' and 'Of the Standard of Taste' (in Hume 1994). A main point is that by actively refining our taste and virtue – which are both broadly aesthetic phenomena for Hume – we appreciate a wider range of subtle and meaningful pleasures. We also, to draw again from the Stoic, derive pleasure from the pursuit of self-refinement itself. For a useful discussion of these and related matters, see Dorsey (2015).

practice philosophy, extend Rizzo and Whitman's intimation that the behavioural economist ought to engage with the public 'as fellow human beings doing the best they can, trying to improve their own choices, and offering friendly advice on how others might do the same' (RW: 439). In doing so, 'behavioral researchers will be less inclined to approach humanity from a position of presumed superiority, like puppet masters correcting the behavior of errant puppets' (ibid.).

Recall the above description of Hume's philosophy involving a shift – which comes forth in 'The Sceptic' – from a perspective of 'I Think' to 'We Do' (from Capaldi 1989: 22). That shift entails a vision of philosophy that de-emphasises foundational metaphysical issues and focuses more on exploring and improving life as it is commonly experienced. The shift moves the locus of philosophy for Hume towards a programme of social science and aesthetics (Hume 2007: 176; for discussion, see Merrill 2015a: 58–61; Matson 2019: 33–36).

The shift has methodological implications. Hume's newfound perspective is a *We* Do' perspective, not an 'Others Do' perspective. The philosopher himself is actuated by the same set of inexplicable habits, feelings and movements of imagination that he observes in others. He is a participant in the social phenomena that he studies; he cannot simply be a detached observer. Understanding himself as a critical participant, the Humean philosopher attempts to cultivate an ethos of humility and self-awareness. This has practical egalitarian implications.[13] Seeing the 'narrow

---

13 Hume's vision of philosophy can perhaps be interpreted as a kind of application of the contemporary idea of analytical egalitarianism, i.e. 'the

and contracted' bounds of his own mind (Hume 1994: 159) – for instance, in his perspectives on the good – the philosopher works to develop a respect for the opinions of others and an openness to conversation and learning. In his intellectual endeavours, he strives to carry himself in the practical, grounded and agreeable manner of an 'honest gentleman' or engaged citizen. He understands himself as fellow traveller of sorts, not an enlightened purveyor of truth (Hume 2007: 177).

---

theoretical system that abstracts from any inherent difference among persons' (Levy and Peart 2008: 1). Not only does Hume assume a universal human nature – an assumption that is central to his 'science of man' – but he quite consciously applies that assumption to *himself* to inform the way in which he studies and participates in society.

Some might contend that Hume is not in fact any sort of analytical egalitarian. Levy and Peart (2004), for instance, emphasise inegalitarian implications of his views of sympathy and approbation in contrast to those of Adam Smith (for a different reading of Hume in relation to Smith on sympathy, see Matson et al. (2019)). One might also flag Hume's disturbingly racist footnote in his essay 'Of National Characters' (Hume 1994: 208, n. 10). That footnote might be taken as evidence that Hume subscribes to a theory of polygenesis. But on a wider reading of Hume's thought, the polygenesis interpretation appears unpersuasive. Kendra Asher presents a compelling case for Hume as a monogeneticist, despite his racist footnote. She even provocatively suggests that the racist footnote itself may have been a complex – though misguided – rhetorical ploy (Asher 2022). Two points along these lines, drawn out in Asher's essay, are worth mentioning. First, Hume excoriates the practice of slavery on moral and economic grounds in his essay 'Of the Populousness of Ancient Nations' (Hume 1994: see especially pp. 387, 396–97). Second, in his essays on commerce he leans heavily on assumptions of a common, universal human nature in explaining economic development, not only in Western Europe, but also in Asia (see 'Of the Rise and Progress of the Arts and Sciences' and 'Of the Balance of Trade' in Hume (1994)). On Hume's reliance in his theorising on a radical 'psychological egalitarianism', see Hundert (1974: 141). See also Schabas's (2021) account of 'the progress of reason' and its explanatory role in Hume's political economy.

The methodological point has a rhetorical dimension: as a fellow traveller and friendly adviser, the philosopher ought to adjust the subject and presentation of his thought so that it is suitable for discourse with his fellows.[14] This rhetorical dimension comes forth both in Hume's personal practice of philosophy and the practice of eighteenth-century philosophy generally.

In eighteenth-century Britain, philosophy took a pragmatic turn. Figures including Richard Steele, Joseph Addison, Jonathan Swift and Alexander Pope – all of whom Hume highly esteemed and imitated throughout his work – perceived in philosophy, when properly cultivated, beneficial potentialities. Philosophical engagement, these intellectuals thought, could help British citizens overcome religious superstition and enthusiasm and usher in a polite age of improvement. But for philosophy to serve this public role, it would need to take on a suitable rhetorical form. Addison and Steele pioneered such a form: the philosophical essay. Philosophical essays were written in an easy, accessible style; such essays brought philosophical insights to bear on matters of day-to-day importance for the citizen. These essays quickly became an essential form of discourse on moral, political, economic, artistic and scientific matters.[15] Alex Benchimol (2010: 46) describes the

---

14 On the connected developments in philosophy and rhetoric in eighteenth-century Britain, see Howell (1971).

15 For further discussion on the philosophical essay and the remarkable scene of voluntary associations in England and Scotland, in which these essays were discussed and debated, see McElroy (1969), Clark (2000), Phillipson (1981) and Habermas (1991).

ethos of this discourse as characterised by 'openness, tolerance, and moral seriousness'; discussion of philosophical essays in England and Scotland approached a 'normative model of critical discourse in the Habermasian sense'.

Hume embraced the philosophical essay.[16] He briefly characterises these efforts in a short piece, 'Of Essay Writing', which was published in 1742 but later withdrawn from his published works. In that essay he fashions himself 'as a Kind of Resident or Ambassador from the Dominions of Learning to those of Conversation.' He takes it as his 'constant Duty to promote a good Correspondence betwixt these two States, which have so great a Dependence on each other.' 'The Materials of this Commerce must chiefly be furnish'd by Conversation and common Life: The manufacturing of them [the materials of social commerce] alone belongs to Learning' (Hume 1994: 535). In other words, as Hume sees it, the philosopher is to mix with the larger body of citizens in order to promote a mutually improving conversation. The philosopher considers matters of interest through participation in day-to-day affairs; he offers reflective interpretations of these affairs, for the sake of understanding and improvement, back to his fellow citizens. In an important sense, then, from this essay we can say that Hume conceived of philosophy as 'a two-way process, paradigmatically embodied in conversation' (Finlay 2007: 63).[17]

---

16 On Hume's literary development and its relation to his philosophy, see Box (1990).

17 For an elaboration of Hume's conception of the philosopher as an 'ambassador', see Livingston (1988).

The understanding of philosophy as a two-way conversation fits nicely with the arc of Hume's happiness essays. From 'The Sceptic', we see that we cannot definitively determine what the good means, how the good life cashes out in context, for different people at different points in time. But we must learn to square that insight with the fact that we genuinely believe that there is a good, that there is meaning in pursuing and reforming our ideas about welfare, and that those ideas have significance for the welfare of others. For Hume, it would seem, we ought to square the insight of 'The Sceptic' with our own convictions of the good by engaging in constructive social discourse, discourse through which we offer our perspectives to others and attempt to persuade, but also through which we are afforded an opportunity to reflect on our own convictions. Hume himself was involved in a number of voluntary associations and clubs that carried on such a discourse for the purpose of personal edification and social improvement. The aim of one club he helped found in 1754, the Edinburgh Select Society, was described in 1755 by the *Scots Magazine*. Its members seek 'by practice to improve themselves in reasoning and eloquence, and by the freedom of debate, to discover the most effectual methods of promoting the good of the country' (quoted in Phillipson 1974: 444). Some of the questions discussed by the society, incidentally, are still today of interest to behavioural economists and policymakers, for example, 'Whether lotteries ought to be encouraged' or 'Whether Whiskie ought not to be laid under such restraints, as to render the use of it less frequent' ('Extract from the Select Society Question Book', n.d.). Not all participants in these discussions, of course, shared Hume's sensibilities. But the mode of philosophy through free debate and conversation for the sake of personal and public improvement is Humean in spirit.

## Conclusion

What are the implications of the Humean method, rhetoric, and public practice of philosophy for behavioural welfare economics? First, when it comes to theorising – and especially formulating policy – about health, wealth and happiness (i.e. welfare), behavioural economists would do well to adopt a more Humean ethos. They should follow the Sceptic in recognising that there is more than one conception of the good life. Although behavioural economists may accept this claim, the understanding that rational behaviour consists in living as if one were a neoclassical economic agent with stable, transitive and context-independent preferences would suggest otherwise. Second, in light of the plurality of good lives to be lived and in light of our inability to define the good for others, behavioural economists ought to view themselves, as Rizzo and Whitman suggest, as 'friendly voices' (RW: 438) in an ongoing conversation. Like Hume, behavioural economists should offer their constructive findings as 'advice columnists' (RW: 438) in a qualified, voluntary manner that seeks to contribute to the well-being of their fellow citizens. Finally, as a rhetorical matter, behavioural economists should present their findings, their psychological and experimental research and theories, as friendly advice directly to their coequal fellow citizens, not as if to a benevolent autocrat (cf. Sugden 2018: 19–23). They should offer their insights up in conversation, as the eighteenth-century Britons did in the coffee houses and drinking clubs of London and Edinburgh and in periodicals such as *The Spectator*, *The Tatler*, *Scots Magazine* and, for a brief time, *The Edinburgh Review*. They should employ argumentative persuasion, not paternalist coercion or subtle manipulation of the choice set through political measures (cf. Hausman and Welch 2010: 130–36). Behavioural economists looking for real-world application of their work would likely be 'equipped with greater humility, greater respect for nonstandard preferences, and greater awareness of the surprising functionality of real-world behavior' (RW: 439).

# REFERENCES

Akerlof, G. A. and Kranton, R. (2000) Economics and identity. *Quarterly Journal of Economics* 115(3): 715–53.

Ambuehl, S., Bernheim, B. D. and Lusardi, A. (2022) Evaluating deliberative competence: a simple method with an application to financial choice. NBER Working Paper 20618 (http://www.nber.org/papers/w20618).

Andreoni, J. and Bernheim, B. D. (2009) Social image and the 50–50 norm: a theoretical and experimental analysis of audience effects. *Econometrica* 77(5): 1607–36.

Angner, E. (2019) We're all behavioral economists now. *Journal of Economic Methodology* 26(3): 195–207.

Asher, K. H. (2021) Moderation and the liberal state: David Hume's history of England. *Journal of Economic Behavior and Organization* 184: 850–59.

Asher, K. H. (2022) Was David Hume a racist? Interpreting Hume's infamous footnote. Part I. *Economic Affairs* 42(2): 225–39.

Ashraf, N., Camerer, C. F. and Loewenstein, G. (2005) Adam Smith, behavioral economist. *Journal of Economic Perspectives* 19(3): 131–45.

Baier, A. (1991) *A Progress of Sentiments: Reflections on Hume's Treatise*. Cambridge, MA: Harvard University Press.

Barry, B. (2010) David Hume as a social theorist. *Utilitas* 22(4): 369–92.

# REFERENCES

Baumol, W. J. (1951) The Neumann–Morgenstern utility index: an ordinalist view. *Journal of Political Economy* 59(1): 61–66.

Bénabou, R. and Tirole, J. (2006) Incentives and prosocial behavior. *American Economic Review* 96(5): 1652–78.

Benchimol, A. (2010) *Intellectual Politics and Cultural Conflict in the Romantic Period: Scottish Whigs, English Radicals and the Making of the British Public Sphere.* Taylor and Francis Group.

Berg, N. (2014) The consistency and ecological rationality approaches to normative bounded rationality. *Journal of Economic Methodology* 21(4): 375–95.

Berg, N. and Gigerenzer, G. (2010) As-if behavioral economics: neoclassical economics in disguise? *History of Economic Ideas* 18(1): 133–65.

Bernheim, B. D. (2016) The good, the bad and the ugly: a unified approach to behavioral welfare economics. *Journal of Benefit-Cost Analysis* 7(1): 12–68.

Bernheim, B. D. (2021) In defense of behavioral welfare economics. *Journal of Economic Methodology* 28(4): 385–400.

Bernheim, B. D. and Rangel, A. (2007) Behavioral public economics: welfare and policy analysis with nonstandard decision-makers. In *Behavioral Economics and Its Applications* (ed. P. Diamond and H. Vartiainen). Princeton University Press.

Beshears, J., Choi, J. J., Laibson, D. and Madrian, B. C. (2008) How are preferences revealed? *Journal of Public Economics* 92: 1787–94.

Besser-Jones, L. (2010) Hume on pride-in-virtue: a reliable motivation? *Hume Studies* 36(2): 171–92.

Binmore, K. (2005) *Natural Justice.* New York: Oxford University Press.

Bleichrodt, H., Pinto, J. L. and Wakker, P. P. (2001) Making descriptive use of prospect theory to improve the prescriptive use of expected utility. *Management Science* 47(11): 1498–514.

Boulding, K. H. (1969) Economics as a moral science. *American Economic Review* 59(1): 1–12.

Bowles, S. (1998) Endogenous preferences: the cultural consequences of markets and other economic institutions. *Journal of Economic Literature* 36: 75–111.

Bowles, S. (2016) *The Moral Economy: Why Good Incentives Are No Substitute for Good Citizens*. New Haven, CT: Yale University Press.

Box, M. A. (1990) *The Suasive Art of David Hume*. Princeton University Press.

Boyd, R. (2008) Manners and morals: David Hume on civility, commerce and the social construction of difference. In *David Hume's Political Economy* (ed. M. Schabas and C. Wennerlind), pp. 65–85. New York: Routledge.

Brown, V. (1992) The dialogic experience of conscience: Adam Smith and the voices of Stoicism. *Eighteenth-Century Studies* 26(2): 233–60.

Brown, V. (1994) *Adam Smith's Discourse: Canonicity, Commerce and Conscience*. London and New York: Routledge.

Buchanan, J. M. (1979) Natural and artifactual man. In *The Logical Foundations of Constitutional Liberty*, vol. 1, pp. 368–73: *The Collected Works of James M. Buchanan*. Indianapolis, IN: Liberty Fund.

Buchanan, J. M. (1999) The relatively absolute absolute. In *The Logical Foundations of Constitutional Liberty*, vol. 1, pp. 442–54. *The Collected Works of James M. Buchanan*. Indianapolis, IN: Liberty Fund.

Buchanan, J. M. (2008) Let us understand Adam Smith. *Journal of the History of Economic Thought* 30(1): 21–28.

Burke, E. (1999 [1790]) Reflections on the revolution in France. Indianapolis, IN: Liberty Fund

Burton, J. H. (1846) *The Life and Correspondence of David Hume* (2 vols), vol. 1. Edinburgh: William Tait.

Camerer, C. F., Issacharoff, S., Loewenstein, G., O'Donoghue, T. and Rabin, M. (2003) Regulation for Conservatives: behavioral economics and the case for 'asymmetric paternalism.' *University of Pennsylvania Law Review* 151: 1211–54.

Camerer, C. F. and Loewenstein, G. (2003) Behavioral economics: past, present and future. In *Advances in Behavioral Economics* (ed. C. F. Camerer, G. Loewenstein and M. Rabin). Princeton University Press.

Campbell, T. D. (1971) *Adam Smith's Science of Morals*. London: George Allen & Unwin.

Capaldi, N. (1989) *Hume's Place in Moral Philosophy*. New York: Peter Lang Publishing.

Cartwright, A. C. and Hight, M. A. (2019) 'Better off as judged by themselves' a critical analysis of the conceptual foundations of nudging. *Cambridge Journal of Economics*, 1–22 (https://doi.org/doi:10.1093/cje/bez012).

Choi, Y. B. (1990) Smith's view on human nature: a problem in the interpretation of 'The Wealth of Nations' and 'The Theory of Moral Sentiments'. *Review of Social Economy* 48(3): 288–302.

Clark, P. (2000) *British Clubs and Societies 1580–1800: The Origins of an Associational World*. Oxford: Clarendon Press.

Colander, D. (2007) Edgeworth's hedonimeter and the quest to measure utility. *Journal of Economic Perspectives* 21(2): 215–25.

Conly, S. (2013) *Against Autonomy: Justifying Coercive Paternalism*. Cambridge University Press.

Danford, J. W. (1990) *David Hume and the Problem of Reason: Recovering the Human Sciences*. New Haven, CT: Yale University Press.

Deci, E. L. and Ryan, R. M. (2008) Hedonia, eudaimonia and well-being: an introduction. *Journal of Happiness Studies* 9(1): 1–11.

Delmotte, C. and Dold, M. (2022) Dynamic preferences and the behavioral case against sin taxes. *Constitutional Political Economy* 33: 80–99.

Den Uyl, D. J. (2016) Impartial spectating and the price analogy. *Econ Journal Watch* 13(2): 264–72.

Dold, M. F. (2018) Back to Buchanan? Explorations of welfare and subjectivism in behavioral economics. *Journal of Economic Methodology* 25(2): 160–78.

Dold, M. F. and Rizzo, M. (2021) Old Chicago against static welfare economics. *Journal of Legal Studies* 50(52): S179–98.

Dold, M. F. and Schubert, C. (2018) Toward a behavioral foundation of normative economics. *Review of Behavioral Economics* 5: 221–41.

Dorsey, D. (2015) Objectivity and perfection in Hume's hedonism. *Journal of the History of Philosophy* 53(2): 245–70.

Drakopoulus, S. A. (2011) Wicksteed, Robbins and the emergence of mainstream economic methodology. *Review of Political Economy* 23(3): 461–70.

Edgell, S. and Tilman, R. (1989) The intellectual antecedents of Thorstein Veblen: a reappraisal. *Journal of Economic Issues* 23(4): 1003–26.

Elster, J. (2016) *Sour Grapes: Studies in the Subversion of Rationality*. New York: Cambridge University Press.

Evensky, J. (1987) The two voices of Adam Smith: moral philosopher and social critic. *History of Political Economy* 19(3): 447–68.

Extract from the Select Society Question Book (n.d.) National Library of Scotland (https://digital.nls.uk/learning/scottish-enlightenment/source/extract-from-the-select-society-question-book/).

Fehr, E. and Hoff, K. (2011) Introduction: tastes, castes and culture: the influence of society on preferences. *Economic Journal* 121(556): 396–412.

Finlay, C. J. (2007) *Hume's Social Philosophy: Human Nature and Commercial Sociability in A Treatise of Human Nature*. London and New York: Continuum International Publishing Group.

Fisher, I. (1892 [1925]) Mathematical investigation in the theory of value and prices. Dissertation, Yale University.

Fleischacker, S. (2004) *On Adam Smith's Wealth of Nations: A Philosophical Companion*. Princeton University Press.

Fleischacker, S. (2016) Adam Smith's impartial spectator: symposium remarks. *Econ Journal Watch* 13 (2): 273–83.

Fleischacker, S. (2019) *Being Me Being You: Adam Smith and Empathy*. University of Chicago Press.

Fogelin, R. J. (1985) *Hume's Skepticism in the Treatise of Human Nature*. London: Routledge and Kegan Paul.

Forbes, D. (1975) *Hume's Philosophical Politics*. Cambridge University Press.

Forman-Barzilai, F. (2010) *Adam Smith and the Circles of Sympathy: Cosmopolitanism and Moral Theory*. Cambridge University Press.

Friedman, M. (1953) The methodology of positive economics. In *Essays in Positive Economics*, pp. 3–43. University of Chicago Press.

Gigerenzer, G. (2010) *Rationality for Mortals*. Oxford University Press.

Griswold, C. L. (1999) *Adam Smith and the Virtues of Enlightenment*. New York: Cambridge University Press.

Grüne-Yanoff, T. and McClennen, E. F. (2008) Hume's framework for a natural history of the passions. In *David Hume's Political Economy* (ed. M. Schabas and C. Wennerlind), pp. 86–104. New York: Routledge.

Gul, F. and Pesendorfer, W. (2010) The case for mindless economics. In *The Foundations of Positive and Normative Economics: A Handbook* (ed. A. Caplin and A. Schotter), pp. 3–39. Oxford University Press.

Haakonssen, K. (1981) *The Science of a Legislator: The Natural Jurisprudence of David Hume and Adam Smith*. Cambridge University Press.

Habermas, J. (1991) *The Structural Transformation of the Public Sphere: An Inquiry into a Category of Bourgeois Society* (trans. T. Burger and F. Lawrence). Cambridge, MA: MIT Press.

Halpern, D. (2015) *Inside the Nudge Unit: How Small Changes Can Make a Big Difference*. Penguin Books.

Hanley, R. P. (2009) *Adam Smith and the Character of Virtue*. Cambridge and New York: Cambridge University Press.

Hardin, R. (2007) *David Hume: Moral and Political Theorist*. New York: Oxford University Press.

Harris, J. A. (2007) Hume's four essays on happiness and their place in the move from morals to politics. *Rivista Di Storia Della Filosofia* 62(3): 223–35.

Hausman, D. (2012) *Preference, Value, Choice and Welfare*. New York: Cambridge University Press.

Hausman, D. M. (2018) Efficacious and ethical public paternalism. *Review of Behavioral Economics* 5: 261–80.

Hausman, D. and Welch, B. (2010) Debate: to nudge or not to nudge. *Journal of Political Philosophy* 18(1): 123–36.

Haybron, D. (2011) Happiness. In *The Stanford Encyclopedia of Philosophy* (ed. E. N. Zalta) (https://plato.stanford.edu/archives/fall2011/entries/happiness/).

Heukelom, F. (2014) *Behavioral Economics: A History*. New York: Cambridge University Press.

Heydt, C. (2007) Relations of literary form and philosophical purpose of Hume's four essays on happiness. *Hume Studies* 33(1): 3–19.

Hirschman, A. O. (2013) *The Passions and the Interests: Political Arguments for Capitalism before Its Triumph*. Princeton Classics Edition. Princeton University Press.

Howell, W. S. (1971) *Eighteenth-Century British Logic and Rhetoric*. Princeton University Press.

Hume, D. (1994) *Essays, Moral, Political and Literary* (ed. E. F. Miller). Indianapolis, IN: Liberty Fund.

Hume, D. (1998 [1751]) *An Enquiry Concerning the Principles of Morals* (ed. T. L. Beauchamp). Oxford: Clarendon Press.

Hume, D. (2000) *An Enquiry Concerning Human Understanding* (ed. T. L. Beauchamp). Oxford: Clarendon Press.

Hume, D. (2007) *A Treatise of Human Nature* (ed. D. F. Norton and M. J. Norton), 2 vols. Oxford University Press.

Hundert, E. J. (1974) The achievement motive in Hume's political economy. *Journal of the History of Ideas* 35(1): 139–43.

Hutcheson, F. (2008 [1725]) *An Inquiry into the Original of Our Ideas of Beauty and Virtue in Two Treatises* (ed. W. Leidhold). Indianapolis, IN: Liberty Fund.

Immerwahr, J. (1989) Hume's essays on happiness. *Hume Studies* 15(2): 307–24.

Immerwahr, J. (1992) Hume on tranquilizing the passions. *Hume Studies* 18(2): 293–314.

Immerwahr, J. (1994) Hume's dissertation on the passions. *Journal of the History of Philosophy* 32(2): 225–40.

Infante, G., Lecouteux, G. and Sugden, R. (2016) Preference purification and the inner rational agent: a critique of the conventional wisdom of behavioural welfare economics. *Journal of Economic Methodology* 23(1): 1–25.

Iyengar, S. S., Huberman, G. and Jiang, W. (2004) How much choice is too much? Contributions to 401(k) retirement plans. In *Pension Design and Structure: New Lessons from Behavioral Finance*, pp. 83–96. Oxford University Press.

Jolls, C. and Sunstein, C. (2006) Debiasing through law. *Journal of Legal Studies* 35(1): 199–242.

Kahneman, D. (2011) *Thinking, Fast and Slow*. New York: Farrar, Straus and Giroux.

Kahneman, D., Diener, E. and Schwarz, N. (eds) (1999) *Well-Being: Foundations of Hedonic Psychology*. New York: Russell Sage Foundation.

Kahneman, D., Knetsch, J. L. and Thaler, R. H. (1991) Anomalies: the endowment effect, loss aversion and status quo bias. *Journal of Economic Perspectives* 5(1): 193–206.

Khalil, E. (2010) Adam Smith's concept of self-command as a solution to dynamic inconsistency and the commitment problem. *Economic Inquiry* 48(1): 177–91.

Klein, D. B. (2004) Statist quo bias. *Econ Journal Watch* 1(2): 260–71.

Klein, D. B., Matson, E. W. and Doran, C. (2018) The man within the breast, the supreme impartial spectator and other impartial spectators in Adam Smith's 'Theory of Moral Sentiments.' *History of European Ideas* 44(8): 1153–68.

Knight, F. (1922) Ethics and the economic interpretation. *Quarterly Journal of Economics* 36(3): 454–81.

Knight, F. (1923) The ethics of competition. *Quarterly Journal of Economics* 37(4): 579–624.

Kőszegi, B. and Rabin, M. (2007) Mistakes in choice-based welfare analysis. *American Economic Review: Papers and Proceedings* 97: 477–81.

Laibson, D. (1997) Golden eggs and hyperbolic discounting. *Quarterly Journal of Economics* 112(2): 443–77.

Levy, D. M. and Peart, S. J. (2004) Sympathy and approbation in Hume and Smith: a solution to the other rational species problem. *Economics and Philosophy* 20: 331–49.

Levy, D. M. and Peart, S. J. (2008) Introduction: the street porter and the philosopher contextualized. In *The Street Porter and the Philosopher: Conversations on Analytical Egalitarianism* (ed. D. M. Levy and S. J. Peart), pp. 1–12. Anne Arbor, MI: University of Michigan Press.

Lewis, D. K. (1969) *Convention: A Philosophical Study.* Cambridge, MA: Harvard University Press.

Lewis, P. and Dold, M. (2020) James Buchanan on the nature of choice: ontology, artifactual man and the constitutional moment in political economy. *Cambridge Journal of Economics* 44(5): 1159–79.

Lichtenstein, S. and Slovic, P. (eds) (2006) *The Construction of Preference.* Cambridge University Press.

Livingston, D. W. (1984) *Hume's Philosophy of Common Life.* University of Chicago Press.

Livingston, D. W. (1988) David Hume: ambassador from the world of learning to the world of conversation. *Political Science Reviewer* 18: 35–84.

Livingston, D. W. (1998) *Philosophical Melancholy and Delirium. Hume's Pathology of Philosophy.* University of Chicago Press.

Loomes, G., Starmer, C. and Sugden, R. (2010) Preference reversals and disparities between willingness to pay and willingness to accept in repeated markets. *Journal of Economic Psychology* 31(3): 374–87.

Marshall, A. (1920 [1890]) *Principles of Economics*, 8th edn. London: Macmillan and Co.

Matson, E. W. (2017) The dual account of reason and the spirit of philosophy in Hume's Treatise. *Hume Studies* 43(2): 29–56 (https://doi.org/10.1353/hms.2017.0009).

Matson, E. W. (2019) Reason and political economy in Hume. *Erasmus Journal for Philosophy and Economics* 12(1): 26–51.

Matson, E. W. (2021a) A dialectical reading of Adam Smith on wealth and happiness. *Journal of Economic Behavior and Organization* 184: 826–36.

Matson, E. W. (2021b) God, commerce and Adam Smith through the editions of The Theory of Moral Sentiments. *Journal of Markets and Morality* 24(2): 269–88.

Matson, E. W. (2021c) Satisfaction in action: Hume's endogenous theory of preferences and the virtues of commerce. *Journal of Economic Behavior and Organization* 183: 849–60.

Matson, E. W. (2022) Our dynamic being within: Smithian challenges to the new paternalism. *Journal of Economic Methodology* 29(4): 309–25.

Matson, E. W. and Dold, M. F. (2021) The behavioral welfare economist in society: considerations from David Hume. *Review of Behavioral Economics* 8(3–4): 239–58.

Matson, E. W. and Klein, D. B. (2022) Convention without convening. *Constitutional Political Economy* 33(1): 1–24.

Matson, E. W., Doran, C. and Klein, D. B. (2019) Hume and Smith on utility, agreeableness, propriety and moral approval. *History of European Ideas* 54(5): 675–704.

McArthur, N. (2007) *David Hume's Political Theory: Law, Commerce and the Constitution of Government*. Toronto University Press.

McArthur, N. (2014) Cosmopolitanism and Hume's general point of view. *European Journal of Political Theory* 13(3): 321–40.

McElroy, D. D. (1969) *Scotland's Age of Improvement: A Survey of Eighteenth-Century Literary Clubs and Societies*. Pullman: Washington State University Press.

McIntyre, J. L. (2000) Hume's passions: direct and indirect. *Hume Studies* 26(1): 77–86.

McKenzie, C. R. M. (2004) Framing effects in inference tasks – and why they are normatively defensible. *Memory and Cognition* 32(6): 874–85.

McRorie, C. (2023.) The anthropology of liberalism: Smith and us. In *Research in the History of Economic Thought and Methodology: Including a Symposium on Religion, The Scottish Enlightenment and the Rise of Liberalism* (ed. L. Fiorito, S. Scheall and C. E. Suprinyak), pp. 79–97. Bingley, UK: Emerald Publishing Limited.

Merrill, T. W. (2015a) *Hume and the Politics of Enlightenment*. New York: Cambridge University Press.

Merrill, T. W. (2015b) Hume's Socratism. *Review of Politics* 77: 23–45.

Mill, J. S. (2003) *On Liberty* (ed. D. Bromwich and G. Kateb). New Haven and London: Yale University Press.

Miller, E. F. (1987) Foreword. In *Essays, Moral, Political and Literary* by D. Hume (ed. E. F. Miller), pp. xi–xviii. Indianapolis, IN: Liberty Fund.

Muller, J. Z. (1993) *Adam Smith in His Time and Ours: Designing the Decent Society*. New York: The Free Press.

O'Donoghue, T. and Rabin, M. (1999) Procrastination in preparing for retirement. In *Behavioral Dimensions of Retirement Economics* (ed. H. J. Aaron), pp. 125–56. Washington DC: Brookings Institution Press.

O'Donoghue, T. and Rabin, M. (2003) Studying optimal paternalism, illustrated by a model of sin taxes. *American Economic Review: Papers and Proceedings* 93(2): 186–91.

Otteson, J. (2002) *Adam Smith's Marketplace of Life*. Cambridge University Press.

Otteson, J. (2018) Adam Smith's libertarian paternalism. In *The Oxford Handbook of Freedom* (ed. D. Schmidtz and C. E. Pavel). Oxford University Press.

Paganelli, M. P. (2010) The moralizing role of distance in Adam Smith: The Theory of Moral Sentiments as possible praise of commerce. *History of Political Economy* 42(3): 425–41.

Paganelli, M. P. (2011) The same face of the two Smith's: Adam Smith and Vernon Smith. *Journal of Economic Behavior and Organization* 78(3): 246–55.

Paganelli, M. P. (2012) David Hume on public credit. *History of Economic Ideas* 20(1): 32–43.

Palacious-Huerta, I. (2003) Time-inconsistent preferences in Adam Smith and David Hume. *History of Political Economy* 35(2): 241–68.

Phillipson, N. (1974) Culture and society in the 18th century province: the case of Edinburgh and the Scottish Enlightenment. In *The University in Society*, vol. II (ed. L. Stone), pp. 407–48. Princeton University Press.

Phillipson, N. (1981) The Scottish Enlightenment. In *The Enlightenment in National Context* (ed. R. Porter and M. Teich), pp. 19–40. Cambridge University Press.

Polanyi, M. (1962) *Personal Knowledge: Towards a Post-Critical Philosophy*. London: Routledge.

Potkay, A. (2000) *The Passion for Happiness. Samuel Johnson and David Hume*. Ithaca and London: Cornell University Press.

Rabin, M. (2002) A perspective on psychology and economics. *European Economic Review* 46(4–5): 657–85.

Railton, P. (1986) Facts and values. *Philosophical Topics* 14(2): 5–31.

Raphael, D. D. (2007) *The Impartial Spectator: Adam Smith's Moral Philosophy*. Oxford: Clarendon Press.

Read, D. and van Leeuwen, B. (1998) Predicting hunger: the effects of appetite and delay on choice. *Organizational Behavior and Human Decision Processes* 76(2): 189–205.

Reed, P. A. (2018) Hume's moral philosophy and contemporary psychology: an overview. In *Hume's Moral Philosophy and Contemporary Psychology* (ed. P. A. Reed and R. Vitz). New York: Routledge.

Reed, P. A. and Vitz, R. (eds) (2018) *Hume's Moral Philosophy and Contemporary Psychology*. New York: Routledge.

Rescher, N. (1987) How serious a fallacy is inconsistency? *Argumentation* 1: 303–16.

Rizzo, M. J. (2017) Rationality – what? Misconceptions of neoclassical and behavioral economics (http://dx.doi.org/10.2139/ssrn.2927443).

Rizzo, M. J. and Whitman, D. G. (2007) Paternalist slopes. *NYU Journal of Law & Liberty* 2: 411–43.

Rizzo, M. J. and Whitman, D. G. (2009) The knowledge problem of new paternalism. *Brigham Young University Law Review* 2009(4): 905–68.

Rizzo, M. J. and Whitman, D. G. (2018) Rationality as a process. *Review of Behavioral Economics* 5(3–4): 201–19.

Rizzo, M. J. and Whitman, D. G. (2020) *Escaping Paternalism: Rationality, Behavioral Economics and Public Policy*. Cambridge University Press.

Rotwein, E. (2009) Introduction. In *Writings on Economics* by D. Hume (ed. E. Rotwein), pp. xxv–cxi. New Brunswick, NJ: Transaction Publishers.

Sabl, A. (2012) *Hume's Politics: Coordination and Crisis in Hume's 'History of England.'* Princeton University Press.

Salant, Y. and Rubinstein, A. (2008) (A, f): Choice with frames. *Review of Economic Studies* 75(4): 1287–96.

Samuelson, P. A. (1938) A note on the pure theory of consumer's behaviour. *Economica* 5(17): 61–71.

Schabas, M. (2014) 'Let your science be human': David Hume and the honourable merchant. *European Journal of the History of Economic Thought* 21(6): 977–90.

Schabas, M. (2021) Hume and 'The Progress of Reason.' *Journal of Economic Behavior and Organization* 183: 874–883.

Schabas, M. and Wennerlind, C. (eds) (2008) *David Hume's Political Economy*. New York: Routledge.

Schafer, K. (2008) Practical reasoning and practical reasons in Hume. *Hume Studies* 34(2): 189–208.

Schelling, T. C. (1980) The intimate contest for self-command. *The Public Interest* 60: 94.

Schliesser, E. (2017) *Adam Smith: Systematic Philosopher and Public Thinker*. New York: Oxford University Press.

Schubert, C. (2015) Opportunity and preference learning. *Economics and Philosophy* 31(2): 275–95.

Sellars, W. (1963) Philosophy and the scientific image of man. In *Science, Perception and Reality*. New York: Routledge & Kegan Paul.

Serdarveric, N. (2021) Choosing less over more money. *Erasmus Journal for Philosophy and Economics* 14(2) (https://doi.org/10.23941/ejpe.v14i2.584).

Simon, H. (1955) A behavioral model of rational choice. *Quarterly Journal of Economics* 69(1): 99–118.

Skinner, A. S. (2009) David Hume: principles of political economy. In *The Cambridge Companion to David Hume* (ed. D. F. Norton and J. Taylor), 2nd edn. Cambridge University Press.

Smith, A. (1981) *An Inquiry into the Nature and Causes of the Wealth of Nations* (ed. R. H. Campbell and A. S. Skinner), 2 vols. Indianapolis, IN: Liberty Fund.

Smith, A. (1982) *The Theory of Moral Sentiments* (ed. D. D. Raphael and A. L. Macfie). Indianapolis, IN: Liberty Fund.

Smith, C. (2016) Peer review and the development of the impartial spectator. *Econ Journal Watch* 13(2): 324–29.

Smith, V. (2003) Constructivist and ecological rationality in economics. *American Economic Review* 93(3): 465–508.

Smith, V. L. and Wilson, B. J. (2019) *Humanomics: Moral Sentiments and the Wealth of Nations for the Twenty-First Century.* New York: Cambridge University Press.

Stewart, M. A. (1991) The Stoic legacy in the early Scottish Enlightenment. In *Atoms, Pneuma and Tranquility: Epicurean and Stoic Themes in European Thought* (ed. M. J. Osler). Cambridge University Press.

Strotz, R. H. (1956) Myopia and inconsistency in dynamic utility maximization. *Review of Economic Studies* 23(3): 165–80.

Sugden, R. (2006) Hume's non-instrumental and non-propositional decision theory. *Economics and Philosophy* 22: 365–91.

Sugden, R. (2017) Do people really want to be nudged towards healthy lifestyles? *International Review of Economics* 64: 113–23.

Sugden, R. (2018) *The Community of Advantage: A Behavioural Economist's Defense of the Market.* Oxford University Press.

Sugden, R. (2021) Hume's experimental psychology and the idea of erroneous preferences. *Journal of Economic Behavior and Organization* 183: 836–48.

Sunstein, C. R. (2020) Behavioral welfare economics. *Journal of Benefit–Cost Analysis* 11(2): 196–220.

Sunstein, C. R. and Thaler, R. H. (2003a) Libertarian paternalism. *American Economic Review* 93(2): 175–79.

Sunstein, C. R. and Thaler, R. H. (2003b) Libertarian paternalism is not an oxymoron. *University of Chicago Law Review* 70(4): 1159–202.

Taylor, J. A. (2015) *Reflecting Subjects: Passion, Sympathy and Society in Hume's Philosophy.* New York: Oxford University Press.

Thaler, R. H. (2016) Behavioral economics: past, present and future. *American Economic Review* 106(7): 1577–600.

Thaler, R. H. and Sunstein, C. R. (2009) *Nudge*, 2nd edn. New York: Penguin Books.

Thoma, J. (2019) Merely means paternalist? Prospect theory and 'debiased' welfare analysis. LSE Choice Group, 30 October (https://www.lse.ac.uk/philosophy/blog/2019/10/30/johanna-thoma-lse-merely-means-paternalist-prospect-theory-and-debiased-welfare-analysis/).

Thoma, J. (2021) On the possibility of an anti-paternalist behavioural welfare economics. *Journal of Economic Methodology* 28(4): 350–63.

Vaggi, G. and Groenewegen, P. (2003) *A Concise History of Economic Thought*. New York: Palgrave Macmillan.

Vanderschraaf, P. (1998) The informal game theory in Hume's account of convention. *Economics and Philosophy* 14: 215–47.

Veblen, T. (1899) Preconceptions of economic science. *Quarterly Journal of Economics* 13(2): 121–50.

Veblen, T. (2007) *The Theory of the Leisure Class: An Economic Study of Institutions* (ed. M. Banta). Oxford University Press.

Viner, J. (1927) Adam Smith and laissez faire. *Journal of Political Economy* 35(2): 198–232.

Vitz, R. (2004) Sympathy and benevolence in Hume's moral psychology. *Journal of the History of Philosophy* 42(3): 261–75.

von Neumann, J. and Morgenstern, O. (2004 [1944]) *Theory of Games and Economic Behavior*, 60th anniversary edition. Princeton University Press.

Vredenburgh, K. (2021) The economic content of a preference. In *The Routledge Handbook of the Philosophy of Economics* (ed. C. Heilmann and J. Reiss), pp. 67–82. Routledge.

Walker, M. (2013) Reconciling the Stoic and the Sceptic: Hume on philosophy as a way of life and the plurality of happy lives. *British Journal for the History of Philosophy* 21(5): 879–901.

Wennerlind Carl (2011) The role of political economy in Hume's moral philosophy. *Hume Studies* 37(1): 43–64.

Whelan, F. G. (1985) *Order and Artifice in Hume's Political Philosophy*. Princeton University Press.

Wincewicz, A. (2018) The aspiring agent: an account of moral personhood for economics. Doctoral dissertation, Newcastle University, Newcastle upon Tyne.

Young, J. T. (1997) *Economics as a Moral Science: The Political Economy of Adam Smith*. Cheltenham and Lyme: Edward Elgar.

# ABOUT THE IEA

The Institute of Economic Affairs is a research and educational charity (No. CC 235 351). Its mission is to improve understanding of the fundamental institutions of a free society by analysing and expounding the role of markets in solving economic and social problems.

The IEA achieves its mission through:

- a high-quality publishing programme
- conferences, seminars, lectures and other events
- outreach to school and university students
- appearances across print, broadcast and digital media

The IEA, established in 1955 by the late Sir Antony Fisher, is an educational charity, not a political organisation. It is independent of any political party or group and does not carry on activities intended to affect support for any political party or candidate in any election or referendum, or at any other time. It is financed by sales of publications, conference fees and voluntary donations.

In addition to its main series of publications, the IEA publishes the academic journal *Economic Affairs* in partnership with the University of Buckingham.

The IEA is aided in its work by an Academic Advisory Council and a panel of Honorary Fellows. Together with other academics, they review prospective IEA publications, their comments being passed on anonymously to authors. All IEA papers are therefore subject to the same rigorous, independent refereeing process as used by leading academic journals.

IEA publications are often used in classrooms and incorporated into school and university courses. They are also sold throughout the world and often translated and reprinted. The IEA supports and works with a global network of like-minded organisations, through its Initiative for African Trade and Prosperity, EPICENTER and other international programmes.

Views expressed in the IEA's publications are those of the authors, not those of the Institute (which has no corporate view), its Managing Trustees, Academic Advisory Council members or senior staff. Members of the Institute's Academic Advisory Council, Honorary Fellows, Trustees and Staff are listed on the following page.

---

The Institute gratefully acknowledges financial support for its publications programme and other work from a generous benefaction by the late Professor Ronald Coase.

**The Institute of Economic Affairs**
2 Lord North Street, Westminster, London SW1P 3LB
Tel: 020 7799 8900
Email: iea@iea.org.uk
Web: iea.org.uk

| Executive Director and Ralph Harris Fellow | Tom Clougherty |
|---|---|
| Editorial Director | Dr Kristian Niemietz |

## Managing Trustees

**Chair:** Linda Edwards

Kevin Bell
Professor Christian Bjørnskov
Robert Boyd
Robin Edwards

Tom Harris
Professor Patrick Minford
Bruno Prior
Professor Martin Ricketts

Lord Vinson – Life Vice President and former Chair of the IEA Board of Trustees
Professor D. R. Myddelton – Life Vice President and Former Chair of the IEA Board of Trustees

## Academic Advisory Council

**Chair:** Professor Martin Ricketts

Dr Mikko Arevuo
Graham Bannock
Dr Roger Bate
Professor Alberto Benegas-Lynch, Jr
Professor Christian Bjørnskov
Professor Donald J Boudreaux
Professor John Burton
Professor Forrest Capie
Dr Juan Castaneda
Professor Steven N S Cheung
Dr Billy Christmas
Professor David Collins
Professor Tim Congdon
Professor Christopher Coyne
Professor David de Meza
Professor Kevin Dowd
Professor David Greenaway
Dr Ingrid A Gregg
Dr Samuel Gregg
Professor Steve H Hanke
Professor Keith Hartley
Professor Peter M Jackson
Dr Jerry Jordan
Professor Syed Kamall
Professor Terence Kealey
Dr Lynne Kiesling
Professor Daniel B Klein
Dr Benedikt Koehler
Dr Mark Koyama
Professor Chandran Kukathas
Dr Tim Leunig
Dr Andrew Lilico
Professor Stephen C Littlechild

Dr Matthew McCaffrey
Professor Ted Malloch
Dr Eileen Marshall
Dr John Meadowcroft
Dr Anja Merz
Dr Lucy Minford
Professor Patrick Minford
Professor Julian Morris
Professor Alan Morrison
Professor D R Myddelton
Dr Marie Newhouse
Dr Chris O'Leary
Paul Ormerod
Dr Neema Parvini
Professor Mark Pennington
Professor Srinivasa Rangan
Dr Alex Robson
Professor Pascal Salin
Dr Razeen Sally
Professor Pedro Schwartz Giron
Professor J R Shackleton
Professor Jane S Shaw Stroup
Professor W Stanley Siebert
Shanker Singham
Professor Andrew Smith
Dr Carlo Stagnaro
Professor Elaine Sternberg
Professor James Tooley
Professor Nicola Tynan
Professor Roland Vaubel
Dr Cento Veljanovski
Professor Lawrence H White
Professor Geoffrey E Wood

## Honorary Fellows

Professor Michael Beenstock
Professor Richard A Epstein
Professor David Laidler

Professor Deirdre McCloskey
Professor Vernon L Smith

*Other books recently published by the IEA include:*

*Capitalism: An Introduction*
Eamonn Butler
ISBN 978-0-255-36758-5; £12.50

*Opting Out: Conscience and Cooperation in a Pluralistic Society*
David S. Oderberg
ISBN 978-0-255-36761-5; £12.50

*Getting the Measure of Money: A Critical Assessment of UK Monetary Indicators*
Anthony J. Evans
ISBN 978-0-255-36767-7; £12.50

*Socialism: The Failed Idea That Never Dies*
Kristian Niemietz
ISBN 978-0-255-36770-7; £17.50

*Top Dogs and Fat Cats: The Debate on High Pay*
Edited by J. R. Shackleton
ISBN 978-0-255-36773-8; £15.00

*School Choice around the World ... And the Lessons We Can Learn*
Edited by Pauline Dixon and Steve Humble
ISBN 978-0-255-36779-0; £15.00

*School of Thought: 101 Great Liberal Thinkers*
Eamonn Butler
ISBN 978-0-255-36776-9; £12.50

*Raising the Roof: How to Solve the United Kingdom's Housing Crisis*
Edited by Jacob Rees-Mogg and Radomir Tylecote
ISBN 978-0-255-36782-0; £12.50

*How Many Light Bulbs Does It Take to Change the World?*
Matt Ridley and Stephen Davies
ISBN 978-0-255-36785-1; £10.00

*The Henry Fords of Healthcare ... Lessons the West Can Learn from the East*
Nima Sanandaji
ISBN 978-0-255-36788-2; £10.00

*An Introduction to Entrepreneurship*
Eamonn Butler
ISBN 978-0-255-36794-3; £12.50

*An Introduction to Democracy*
Eamonn Butler
ISBN 978-0-255-36797-4; £12.50

*Having Your Say: Threats to Free Speech in the 21st Century*
Edited by J. R. Shackleton
ISBN 978-0-255-36800-1; £17.50

*The Sharing Economy: Its Pitfalls and Promises*
Michael C. Munger
ISBN 978-0-255-36791-2; £12.50

*An Introduction to Trade and Globalisation*
Eamonn Butler
ISBN 978-0-255-36803-2; £12.50

*Why Free Speech Matters*
Jamie Whyte
ISBN 978-0-255-36806-3; £10.00

*The People Paradox: Does the World Have Too Many or Too Few People?*
Steven E. Landsburg and Stephen Davies
ISBN 978-0-255-36809-4; £10.00

*An Introduction to Economic Inequality*
Eamonn Butler
ISBN 978-0-255-36815-5; £10.00

*Carbon Conundrum: How to Save Climate Change Policy from Government Failure*
Philip Booth and Carlo Stagnaro
ISBN 978-0-255-36812-4; £12.50

*Scaling the Heights: Thought Leadership, Liberal Values and the History of The Mont Pelerin Society*
Eamonn Butler
ISBN 978-0-255-36818-6; £10.00

*Faith in Markets? Abrahamic Religions and Economics*
Edited by Benedikt Koehler
ISBN 978-0-255-36824-7; £17.50

*Human Nature and World Affairs: An Introduction to Classical Liberalism and International Relations Theory*
Edwin van de Haar
ISBN 978-0-255-36827-8; £15.00

*The Experience of Free Banking*
Edited by Kevin Dowd
ISBN 978-0-255-36830-8; £25.00

*Apocalypse Next: The Economics of Global Catastrophic Risks*
Stephen Davies
ISBN 978-0-255-36821-6; £17.50

## Other IEA publications

Comprehensive information on other publications and the wider work of the IEA can be found at www.iea.org.uk. To order any publication please see below.

## Personal customers

Orders from personal customers should be directed to the IEA:

IEA
2 Lord North Street
Westminster
London SW1P 3LB
Tel: 020 7799 8911
Email: accounts@iea.org.uk

## Trade customers

All orders from the book trade should be directed to the IEA's distributor:

Ingram Publisher Services UK
1 Deltic Avenue
Rooksley
Milton Keynes MK13 8LD
Tel: 01752 202301
Email: ipsuk.orders@ingramcontent.com

## IEA subscriptions

The IEA also offers a subscription service to its publications. For a single annual payment (currently £42.00 in the UK), subscribers receive every monograph the IEA publishes. For more information please contact:

Subscriptions
IEA
2 Lord North Street
Westminster
London SW1P 3LB
Tel: 020 7799 8911
Email: accounts@iea.org.uk